GREAT WAR LITERATURE

STUDY GUIDE

Written by W Lawrance

on

FIRST WORLD WAR
PLAYS

Great War Literature Study Guide on First World War Plays
Written by W Lawrance

Published by:
Great War Literature Publishing LLP
Darrington Lodge, Springfield Road, Camberley, Surrey GU15 1AB Great Britain
Web site: www.greatwarliterature.co.uk
E-Mail: editor@greatwarliterature.co.uk

Produced in Great Britain

Published March 2007. Copyright ©Wendy Lawrance 2007.
The moral right of the author has been asserted.

ISBN 978-1905378418 (1905378416) Paperback Revised Edition - October 2006

10 9 8 7 6 5 4 3 2 1

First published in Paperback March 2007
First published as e-Book March 2007

Design and production by Great War Literature Publishing LLP
Typeset in Gill Sans and Trajan Pro

Great War Literature Study Guide on

First World War Plays

CONTENTS

List of Illustrations   7
Acknowledgements   9

Preface   11

Journey's End by R C Sherriff   13
Introduction   13
Synopsis   15
    Act One   15
    Act Two   19
    Act Three   23
Glossary of Terms   27
Characters   29
    Stanhope   29
    Raleigh   35
    Osborne   39
    Trotter   43
    Hibbert   45
    Mason   47
    Hardy   48
Historical Significance   49
Portrayal of the Ranks in the British Army   53
R.C. Sherriff - Biography   59
Themes   61
    Futility and Waste   61
    Boredom and Tension   64
    Schooldays and Heroes   67
    Family   71
    Humour   73
Comparisons   75
    Male Relationships   75
    The Effects of the War on the Individual   82

The Effects of Death and Loss on the Individual   86
Responsibility   91
A Question of Comparisons   93
The Effects of War on the Individual   93
The Presentation of Heroism   95
The Effects of War on Male Relationships   97

The Accrington Pals by Peter Whelan   101
Introduction   101
Synopsis   103
Act One   103
Act Two   111
Characters   117
May Hassal   117
Tom Hackford   121
CSM Rivers   123
Minor Characters   125
History of the Accrington Pals   127
The Battle of the Somme   131
Themes   135
Sacrifice   135
Changing Times   138
Relationships   141
Comparisons   145
Effects of War   145
Portrayal of Women   147
Faith   150
A Question of Comparisons   153
The Changing Role of Women   153
Portrayal of Friendships in War   154

Not About Heroes by Stephen MacDonald   157
Introduction   157
Synopsis   159
Act One   159
Act Two   164
Biographies   169
Siegfried Sassoon   169

Wilfred Owen   176
Robert Graves   181
Robbie Ross   187
Edward Marsh   191
H. G. Wells   192
Arnold Bennett   193
Themes   195
Males Relationships   195
Feelings about the War   198
Comparison   201
Fact in Fiction - A Critical Assessment   201

Oh What a Lovely War
by Joan Littlewood's Theatre Workshop   209
Introduction   209
Synopsis   211
Act One   211
Act Two   213
Biographies   215
Douglas Haig   215
John French   220
Critical Analysis   227
Portrayal of Characters   227
The Representation of the War   231
Comparison   237
The Use of Satire in First World War Literature   237

Appendix - Ranks in the British Army during the
First World War   242
Further Reading Recommendations for A-Level Students   245
General Advice to Students   250
Bibliography   251
Other Titles   255

LIST OF ILLUSTRATIONS

Journey's End by R C Sherriff

Copy of *Journey's End*, signed by the author R C Sherriff,
producers Maurice Browne, Gilbert Miller, James F Reilly and
Bertram Harrison, director and scenic designer James Whale
and the cast of the first production in March 1929 at the
Henry Miller Theatre, New York.   14

Plaster-cast by Jane Jackson, showing the original
set-design for *Journey's End*.   18

Maurice Browne, Producer, with members of the
original cast for *Journey's End*, Savoy Theatre,
21 January 1929.   34

Cast list from the *Journey's End* programme at the
Savoy Theatre 1929.   42

General Henri-Philippe Pétain and Marshal Ferdinand Foch   50

The ruins of St Quentin   51

Entrance to St Quentin Canal   51

R C Sherriff obituary   58

The Accrington Pals by Peter Whelan

Saturday 26th September 1914: The Battalion, led by
Col R Sharples and the 'Accrington Old Band', parades
through Accrington town centre before the Mayor
and raiser of the Battalion, John Harwood JP.   102

June 1915: Pals marching through Accrington Centre
past the Town Hall and the Mayor, in full regalia.   116

Pals relaxing at Rugeley Camp   137

Not About Heroes by Stephen MacDonald

Publicity Still from the production of Not About Heroes
performed at Barons Court Theatre, 2005.   158

Production of Not About Heroes, performed at Barons
Court Theatre, 2005.   166

Inscription on the tombstone of Siegfried Sassoon,
St Andrew's Church, Mells.   168

St Andrew's Church, Mells, Somerset.   175

Oh What a Lovely War
by Joan Littlewood's Theatre Workshop

Field Marshal Sir Douglas Haig   215

Field Marshal Sir John French   220

ACKNOWLEDGEMENTS

I would like to express my gratitude to all of those involved in the preparation of this book. These include: Yvonne Widger of The Dartington Hall Trust Archive (www.dartingtonarchive.org.uk); Dov Martin of M.A.D. House Plays (www.madhouseplays.com); Dr Peter Thwaites, Curator Sandhurst Collection at the Royal Military Academy Sandhurst (www.sandhurst.mod.uk); Andrew Orgill, Librarian, Royal Military Academy Sandhurst (www.sandhurst.mod.uk); Catherine Duckworth, Accrington Local Studies Library (www.lancashire.gov.uk/libraries/services/local/accrington.asp); Helen Hargest, of the The Shakespeare Centre Library, The Shakespeare Birthplace Trust (www.shakespeare.org.uk); Jane Davies, Curator, Museum of the Queen's Lancashire Regiment (www.army.mod.uk/qlr/museum_archives/index.htm).

The opinions expressed in this book in no way reflect the opinions of the people or organisations mentioned above.

Every endeavour has been made to contact copyright holders where applicable. Apologies are offered to those copyright holders whom it has proved impossible to locate.

PREFACE

Great War Literature Study Guides' primary purpose is to provide in-depth analysis of First World War literature for A-Level students.

There are plenty of other study guides available and while these make every effort to help with the analysis of war literature, they do so from a more general overview perspective.

Great War Literature Publishing have taken the positive decision to produce a more detailed and in-depth interpretation of selected works for students. We also actively promote the publication of our works in an electronic format via the Internet to give the broadest possible access.

Our publications can be used in isolation or in collaboration with other study guides. It is our aim to provide assistance with your understanding of First World War literature, not to provide the answers to specific questions. This approach provides the resources that allow the student the freedom to reach their own conclusions and express an independent viewpoint.

Great War Literature Study Guides can include elements such as biographical detail, historical significance, character assessment, synopsis of text, and analysis of poetry and themes, together with critical assessments of various aspects of a piece.

The structure of Great War Literature Study Guides allows the reader to delve into a required section easily without the need to read from beginning to end. This is especially true of our e-Books.

The Great War Literature Study Guides have been thoroughly researched and are the result of over 25 years of experience of studying this particular genre.

Students must remember that studying literature is not about being right or wrong, it is entirely a matter of opinion, and that the viewpoints expressed in this study guide are just that: opinion. The secret to success for a student, however, is to develop the ability to form these opinions and to deliver them succinctly and reinforce them with quotes and clear references from the text.

Great War Literature Study Guides will help to extend your knowledge of First World War literature and offer clear definitions and guidance to enhance your studying. Our clear and simple layouts make the guides easy to access and understand.

JOURNEY'S END
BY R. C. SHERRIFF

INTRODUCTION

This play was originally performed in December 1928 and published the following year. The action takes place in a dugout, in a British trench near St Quentin in France. This is a story of the relationships between five officers between 18th and 21st March 1918, immediately prior to a major battle.

We experience everything from mundane discussions regarding the merits of pineapple over apricots, to the death of one of the officers and the impact this has on those left behind.

There are many moments of humour in the play, particularly at the beginning, which serve to intensify the horrors which the men are experiencing. By introducing humour and detailed personalities into the play, Sherriff demonstrates the human cost of the war which destroyed a generation of young men, the like of which would never be seen again.

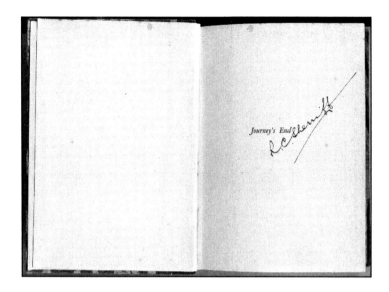

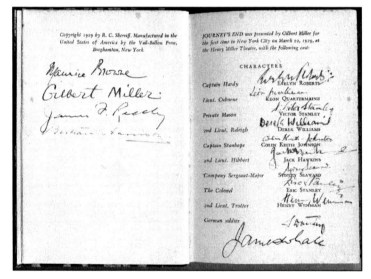

Copy of *Journey's End*, signed by the author R C Sherriff (top), producers Maurice Browne, Gilbert Miller, James F Reilly and Bertram Harrison, director and scenic designer James Whale and the cast of the first production in March 1929 at the Henry Miller Theatre, New York (bottom).
Image courtesy of The Dartington Hall Trust Archive.

SYNOPSIS

ACT ONE

The play opens with Captain Hardy, alone in the dugout, trying to dry his sock, while singing a song to himself. Osborne arrives and the two men share a drink while Hardy finishes dressing. Hardy's regiment is being replaced at the front by Osborne's and the two men discuss what has been happening lately, and the likelihood of a German attack. They talk about the layout and condition of the dugout and trenches and Hardy hands over a list of supplies. The conversation turns to Stanhope - Osborne's company commander. Hardy appears critical of Stanhope's drinking, but Osborne defends him. Although Hardy should really wait and hand over to Stanhope personally, he chooses not to and leaves Osborne to pass on his messages.

The officers' servant - a soldier named Mason - appears and he and Osborne discuss that night's meal. Raleigh arrives: he is a new officer, fresh from England. Osborne welcomes him and, over a drink, it soon becomes clear that Raleigh already knows Stanhope. He explains that they had been at the same school, although Stanhope is three years older. Raleigh's devotion to his old school friend is obvious - in fact it would seem that Raleigh has used some of his family's influence to ensure that he would be assigned to Stanhope's Company. He reveals that Stanhope and his sister share a close friendship, a fact of which Osborne had not previously been aware. Osborne seems concerned that Raleigh might notice some changes in Stanhope and tries to prepare him, as well as explaining some of the routine of the dugout and the trenches.

Raleigh is introduced to Mason, who is worried because a tin which he thought contained pineapple chunks, turns out to be full of apricots and he knows that Stanhope dislikes this particular fruit. Osborne tries to reassure him. Just then Stanhope arrives, together with Second Lieutenant Trotter. Stanhope is angry about the condition of the trenches and orders Mason to bring him some whisky. When he is introduced to Raleigh, Stanhope is shocked to see him and an uneasy atmosphere descends, which Osborne tries his best to cover up.

Raleigh is introduced to Trotter and the men sit down to eat, although Stanhope becomes angry once more when they discover that there is no pepper to go with their soup. While they eat, they discuss their position and their duties for that night. Raleigh is sent on duty with Trotter as it is his first time in the trenches. The man they have relieved - Hibbert - enters the dugout, declines any food and, complaining of a pain in his eye, goes straight to bed. Stanhope seems to think that Hibbert is faking his illness and is unsympathetic. Osborne turns the conversation to Raleigh and Stanhope expresses his surprise that of all the Companies in France, Raleigh should have been sent to his. He shows Osborne a photograph of Raleigh's sister and tells him how concerned he is at how much his personality has changed and how frightened he is.

Stanhope reveals his fear that Raleigh will write to his sister, Madge and reveal the truth about his drinking. Then he realises that he could censor Raleigh's letters and continue to keep his drinking a secret. By now Stanhope is quite drunk and very tired, so Osborne persuades him to sleep for a while, and then retires to bed himself.

Main Points of Interest in Act One

HARDY'S ROLE
- Introduces humour right at the beginning of the play which sets the tone.
- Sets the scene by describing the surroundings, boredom and hardships in the dugout.
- Provides background information on Stanhope's character.

RALEIGH'S ARRIVAL
- Revealing conversation with Osborne regarding Stanhope's pre-war personality which differs greatly from Hardy's description.
- Raleigh's innocence and nervousness contrast with Hardy and Osborne who are more experienced and resigned to their situation.

MEETING BETWEEN RALEIGH AND STANHOPE
- Stanhope is shocked by Raleigh's arrival in his Company and reacts awkwardly.
- Raleigh's attempts at conversation are rejected by Stanhope.

STANHOPE'S CONVERSATION WITH OSBORNE
- Stanhope's resentment of Raleigh's presence becomes clear.
- He reveals his relationship with Madge to Osborne, showing that he trusts his friend more than Raleigh, with whom he has barely spoken.
- We learn of Stanhope's assessment of his own weaknesses and his fears for the future.

STANHOPE'S RELATIONSHIP WITH OSBORNE
- It is clear that Stanhope is closer to Osborne than to anyone else, including Raleigh.

- Stanhope is portrayed as 'childlike' and needy, while Osborne is seen as the 'father-figure' which is the opposite role to their ranks and experience.
- The audience learn how vital Osborne is to the Company as a whole and Stanhope in particular

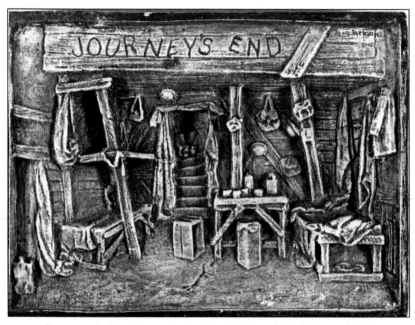

Plaster-cast by Jane Jackson, showing the original set-design for *Journey's End.*
Image courtesy of The Dartington Hall Trust Archive.

ACT TWO

It is the following morning and Stanhope is on duty in the trench, while the other men are eating breakfast in the dugout. They talk about Stanhope, who they think looks unwell, although Raleigh seems embarrassed by the tone of the conversation and is reluctant to criticise his old friend. Sensing Raleigh's discomfort, Osborne changes the subject and they talk about the weather and gardening until Trotter goes to relieve Stanhope. Left by themselves for a short while, Osborne tells Raleigh that he used to play rugby for Harlequins and England, which impresses the younger man. They also discuss the war in general, although when Stanhope returns, Raleigh excuses himself and goes back to his own dugout to finish a letter.

Osborne and Stanhope talk over their immediate tasks, such as repairing the barbed wire, and also the anticipated German attack. Although it is only early in the morning, Stanhope starts drinking. He is very worried about Raleigh's letter and when he reappears with it, ready for posting, Stanhope tells him that he must leave it open on the table so that it can be censored. Raleigh is flustered and initially refuses to show his letter, saying that he will leave it until later. This fuels Stanhope's fears and he wrenches the letter from Raleigh's hand in a violent outburst. Raleigh is shocked by his friend's behaviour and quietly leaves the dugout to go on duty. Osborne is also stunned, but Stanhope turns on him too, before realising that his actions were unnecessarily harsh. He no longer wants to read the letter and throws it down on the table. Osborne offers to glance at it, just to set Stanhope's mind at rest and reads it quietly to himself. When he has finished, he offers to tell Stanhope what Raleigh has said and, although he dreads hearing it, Stanhope agrees. Osborne reads part of Raleigh's letter aloud, which reveals that he feels honoured to be serving with Stanhope; that Stanhope is always tired, but that this is because he is such a good officer who rarely sleeps and is always trying to cheer up the men, and also that the men love him. Ralcigh is full of pride that Stanhope is *his* friend. Osborne sticks down the envelope and Stanhope stands, ashamed now that he had doubted Raleigh.

Later that day, Stanhope is issuing instructions to a Sergeant-Major when the Colonel arrives. The Sergeant-Major is excused and then the Colonel reveals that he wants Stanhope to organise a raiding party to be sent across No Man's Land to capture one or two enemy soldiers, in the hope of discovering the strength of the opposition. The Colonel suggests that Osborne should lead the raid and be supported by Raleigh. Stanhope tries to convince the Colonel that Raleigh is too inexperienced, but eventually it is agreed that there is no-one else who could go and the Colonel leaves.

Hibbert appears, having been asleep. He says he feels too unwell to remain at the front. Stanhope tells him that he is suffering from the same complaint himself, but Hibbert persists, saying that he wants to leave the front line and go for medical assistance. Stanhope stops him and says that he will not be allowed to leave: he is not *that* unwell. Hibbert becomes hysterical and goes to collect his belongings, saying that he is going to leave anyway. Stanhope fetches his revolver and, when Hibbert returns and tries to leave the dugout, a heated argument follows during which Hibbert tries to hit Stanhope, who becomes angry and tells Hibbert that, rather than allow him to leave, he would shoot him and make it look like an accident. Hibbert tells him to go ahead - he would rather be shot than have to spend one more moment in the trenches. The two men face each other and eventually, Stanhope replaces his revolver and speaks quietly to Hibbert, telling him how frightened he is. He appeals to Hibbert not to let his comrades down and somehow persuades him to stay, offering to go on duty with him to help calm his nerves.

Osborne comes into the dugout and Stanhope tells him that he is to lead the raid. Stanhope leaves to make arrangements with the Sergeant-Major and a sleepy Trotter appears from his bed. Osborne tells him about the raid and they agree not to discuss the details in front of Raleigh in case he becomes frightened. Osborne is reading *Alice's Adventures in Wonderland* and Trotter seems surprised by his choice of book, although he has never read it himself.

Stanhope returns and collects Hibbert, taking him out into the trench. Osborne and Trotter settle down to some letter writing and Raleigh comes off duty, having been relieved by Stanhope and Hibbert. He has been told about the raid, and is very excited, viewing it as an adventurous opportunity.

Main Points of Interest in Act Two

CHARACTERS

- The audience learns more about Trotter and his background as well as what the others think about him.
- Stanhope wonders about his own sanity and is, once again, reassured by Osborne.
- We discover that Osborne has a family at home. Later in the scene, he demonstrates his loyalty to the Company.

THE LETTER

- Raleigh's reluctance to show his letter to Stanhope stems from his embarrassment at what he has written in praise of his hero.
- Stanhope's misinterpretation of this and his violent outburst reveal the extent of his paranoia.
- The contents of Raleigh's letter show his loyalty towards his old friend, as well as the high opinion in which Stanhope is held by his men. This shows us that Stanhope is much harsher towards himself than others.

THE COLONEL'S VISIT

- Brings the first news of the raid.
- Stanhope's reaction to the suggestion that Raleigh should go on the raid is interesting. He doesn't flinch when told Osborne is going, but tries several times to have Raleigh excused from this duty. This could suggest that he still feels responsible for Raleigh's welfare, or that he knows Raleigh's inexperience could prove costly.

STANHOPE'S ARGUMENT WITH HIBBERT

- Stanhope is portrayed as loyal, devoted to the whole Company and with high expectations of others, but ultimately sympathetic.
- Hibbert is shown as only interested in saving his own skin, but when this fails, his sole concern is that no-one should discover his weakness.

ACT THREE

It is the following afternoon and Stanhope is nervously pacing the floor of the dugout, when the Colonel arrives. The two men discuss the plans for the raid. When Osborne and Raleigh come in, the Colonel offers them words of encouragement. Once Osborne and Stanhope are alone, Osborne asks Stanhope to take care of his personal effects, just in case he does not come back from the raid. Stanhope says he will do this, but refuses to acknowledge that Osborne might not return. Finally, Raleigh and Osborne are alone and they go over what will happen during the raid. Then they try to talk about anything else *except* the raid, until eventually the time comes for them to leave. Raleigh suddenly seems nervous, but Osborne calms him down. They leave the dugout, which remains empty, although the noise of the raid can be heard.

When all has gone quiet, Stanhope and the Colonel come into the dugout from the trench. The raid has resulted in the capture of one German soldier who is brought down into the dugout. Stanhope goes back out to talk to the men, while the Colonel interrogates the prisoner. Stanhope returns and the Colonel absent-mindedly asks whether all the men have returned safely, to which Stanhope replies, bitterly, that Osborne and six others have been killed. Raleigh enters the dugout and, after congratulating him, the Colonel leaves. Raleigh sits, dumbfounded and in shock, on Osborne's bed. Stanhope has no words of consolation, but simply asks why he must sit there, rather than somewhere else.

Later that evening, Trotter, Stanhope and Hibbert, having dined, sit and tell stories and jokes. This has been a special dinner including chicken and champagne, but Raleigh has chosen to remain on duty in the trench, rather than join them. Hibbert reveals that Raleigh did not want to come to the dinner and preferred to be with the men. This news shakes Stanhope, who becomes angry and orders

Hibbert to go to bed. Once they are alone, Stanhope tells Trotter that he is now second-in-command. Trotter promises not to disappoint Stanhope, and goes out to relieve Raleigh.

When Raleigh enters, Stanhope is angry with him for not attending the dinner and Raleigh makes matters worse by admitting that he has eaten with the men. Stanhope's temper becomes almost uncontrollable and Raleigh is confused, not just by Stanhope's attitude, but also about why they all had a celebratory meal when Osborne had just been killed. Stanhope angrily explains that the drinking and celebration are done to forget, not because he does not care. He dismisses Raleigh.

Very early the next morning, the officers wake up and prepare for the expected attack. Mason is told that he will have to join his platoon in the trench once he has completed his chores. The Sergeant-Major comes down to the dugout to get his instructions. Trotter comes out and calls for Raleigh and Hibbert to join him, before going out into the trench. Raleigh appears and pauses to say goodbye to Stanhope, who barely acknowledges him. Hibbert still has not appeared, so Stanhope calls him again, but when he does come out, he is reluctant to go into the trench. Eventually, Stanhope finds a way around the situation by asking Hibbert to accompany Mason into the trenches. Hibbert can hardly refuse this order and the two men leave. Various messages come down for Stanhope and he gets ready to go up himself. The Sergeant-Major comes down to tell him that Raleigh has been wounded. Stanhope tells him to bring Raleigh down to the dugout and, despite his surprise, the Sergeant-Major obeys and carries Raleigh to Osborne's bed. Raleigh has been badly wounded and Stanhope bathes his head. The two men talk briefly, although Raleigh does not understand the extent of his injuries. Stanhope conceals the truth from him and reassures him that he will be fine. Their friendship is restored as Stanhope briefly takes care of Raleigh in the few minutes before he dies.

A soldier comes down into the dugout and says that Trotter has asked for Stanhope to come up immediately. Stanhope pauses to touch Raleigh's head, before going up into the trench. Just as he does, a shell bursts just outside and the entrance caves in, extinguishing the one remaining candle. All is in darkness and the only sound is of the shells and machine-gun fire.

Main Points of Interest in Act Three

BEFORE THE RAID
- Stanhope's anxiety and sense of foreboding are clear.
- Osborne's and Stanhope's parting is a mixture of restraint and unspoken emotional intensity which sums up the difference between pre-war male roles and the close relationships that were formed during the conflict.
- Osborne's conversation with Raleigh demonstrates, once again, his importance to the Company.

AFTER THE RAID
- Osborne's death, by hand grenade as he waited for Raleigh, makes Stanhope bitter and angry as well as sad and reflective.
- Raleigh seeks help from Stanhope but is rejected. This may reflect Stanhope's feelings that Raleigh is somehow responsible for Osborne's death, or the fact that Stanhope simply cannot cope with someone else's grief and emotions.

THE DINNER
- Stanhope clearly does not want to talk about the raid, he wants to forget.
- Hibbert appears to be only concerned with having a good time - he has misinterpreted the reason behind the dinner.
- Stanhope's extreme anger towards Raleigh and his description of his feelings for Osborne show the audience how moved he really is to have lost his friend.

RECONCILIATION BETWEEN STANHOPE AND RALEIGH
- When Raleigh is wounded, Stanhope's insistence that he be brought to the dugout, his tender care for the dying man and, for the first time, his use of Raleigh's christian name all show how Stanhope really feels.
- Stanhope's character is restored and we glimpse his pre-war personality in this fleeting scene.

GLOSSARY OF TERMS

Some of the military language and terminology used in Journey's End can be confusing. We have included below a list of some of the terms or phrases from the play which may require explanation, in alphabetical order.

Billets - Lodging for a soldier, normally in private homes, farm outhouses or public buildings.

Boche - French slang for a German, also adopted by the British.

Dugout - A shelter dug underground. In the First World War, officers at the front essentially lived in these constructions which were sometimes joined together by a series of tunnels.

Funk - Fear or terror.

Lanyard - A cord worn around the waist or neck to secure a gun, knife or whistle.

Lewis Gun - A type of machine gun, used by the British during the First World War.

Log-book - The official record of what has taken place in a particular sector.

MC - Abbreviation for Military Cross. Established in December 1914, this medal was awarded for gallantry to officers, up to the rank of Captain, although it has since been expanded to include other ranks.

Minnies - A German trench mortar, actually named a 'Minenwerfer' which literally translates as 'mine-launcher'.

No Man's Land - Area of land between the front line trenches.

Parapet - The part of the trench which faces No Man's Land, raised to protect the men from enemy fire.

Pavé - French for a type of pavement, usually made of square cobbles, used on older roads.

Quartermaster-Sergeant - A senior non-commissioned officer who is responsible for supplies.

Sap - A communication trench dug at an angle from the main trench system.

Sentry Post - Position where a man could be positioned to stand guard or observe enemy activity.

Toch-emmas - Army slang for a trench mortar.

Trench Fever - A disease which was quite common in the First World War, causing high fever, headache and back or leg pain. It was transmitted by the lice that infested the men's clothing.

Very Lights - A flare fired from a gun.

Whizzbangs - Slang name used by the British for German artillery. Refers to the noise made by the travelling shell, followed by the explosion.

Wipers - Slang for the Belgian town of Ypres, which saw intense fighting throughout the First World War.

CHARACTERS

STANHOPE

The son of a country vicar, this young captain is the commanding officer of the company of men with whom Journey's End is concerned. Aged approximately twenty-one years, Stanhope has been in the trenches for almost three years, having gone into the army at eighteen. Physically, he is described as tall, thin, and having broad shoulders. The impression created is that he is fastidious about his appearance, having neatly brushed dark hair and a well-cared-for uniform. The description given of Stanhope also refers to the effects of serving in France for three years: although tanned, his face is pale and he appears very tired and drawn.

Even before his first appearance, the conversation between Osborne and Hardy has already made it clear that Stanhope drinks heavily and through the course of the play, we learn that this is done to boost his nerves, which even he appreciates, are shattered. The alcohol also helps him to forget the horrors of everyday trench life and death. This early conversation tells us much more about Stanhope; for example he is fussy about the cleanliness of the trenches. Stanhope likes the trenches and dugouts to be well maintained and with good reason: ammunition stored improperly in wet or damp trenches can go rusty and malfunction; disease can easily be spread amongst the men due to poor sanitation; and he resents the idea of his men, who already have sufficient tasks to keep them occupied, having to spend their time clearing up someone else's mess. To Stanhope, such inefficiency is intolerable. During this same conversation we also discover the high regard in which Stanhope is held. Osborne comments to Hardy that he does not know of anyone who is as good a commander as Stanhope and we learn how much Osborne loves him. Stanhope is obviously an excellent officer, and has been awarded the MC, so his courage is not in doubt to anyone except himself. He is concerned with the welfare of his men: but this concern, together with his experiences and fears have taken their toll on him both physically and mentally. He is a man on the verge of breaking down.

When his old friend Raleigh appears in his Company, Stanhope is shocked and he finds it difficult to disguise this. Ever since they were at school together Stanhope has always regarded it as his responsibility to look after Raleigh, particularly as their fathers were old friends. Now his task is harder than ever - taking care of a younger boy at school, and living up to his high expectations is completely different from looking after a junior officer in the front line trenches. He is also aware that Raleigh has always hero-worshiped him, and he is afraid of losing Raleigh's respect once it becomes clear how drastically different he has become.

He would prefer it if Raleigh had been able to remember him as a boy-hood hero, than a broken man, which is how Stanhope now perceives himself. In addition he is also concerned that in writing home, Raleigh will betray Stanhope's altered nature and that this might not only shatter his image within his own family, but also with Raleigh's sister Madge, who he obviously loves and with whom he has an understanding. He is keen that Raleigh's sister should be proud of him, and never know of the ways in the which the war has changed him. It is also possible that Stanhope is finding it almost impossible to reconcile his pre-war life with his wartime existence. Seeing Raleigh simply reminds him of a life he has left behind. Watching Raleigh's reactions to the changed Stanhope also reinforces Stanhope's opinion that he is become so badly affected by the war that he will be unrecognisable afterwards.

Stanhope's outburst when Raleigh refuses to hand over his letter is extreme and shocks his young friend, as well as Osborne, who has clearly never seen Stanhope behave in this way before. However, Stanhope soon realises that he has behaved badly and his reaction to the content of Raleigh's letter shows how ashamed he is of his own shortcomings. This episode also demonstrates to the audience that, despite his own poor opinion of himself, Stanhope is still essentially a decent man.

Stanhope is conscious of the impression he creates with his men and junior officers and the only person allowed to see him with his guard down is Osborne. Stanhope is very critical of himself but his opinion of his own shortcomings is not reflected by the men in his own Company, who, despite his obvious problems, continue to look up to and respect him. This is not a universally-held opinion, as we have already learned from Hardy that some of the men from outside his company regard Stanhope's behaviour as somewhat freakish or laughable, especially when he is drunk. This may be, however, because it is easier for them to laugh at him than to appreciate that what has happened to him could just as easily happen to them.

We also see that Stanhope is a man with a strong sense of duty: while discussing plans with the Sergeant-Major, he suggests that, rather than retreat in the face of the enemy, the company will continue to go forward until they have won the war! This is said half-humourously - Stanhope obviously has no intention of retreating - it would be contrary to his orders, but also he wants to reassure the Sergeant-Major who seems to be worried about the strength of the anticipated attack.

Hibbert's supposed illness demonstrates another side of Stanhope, who makes it clear that he will do whatever it takes for the good of his Company. This becomes clear in the episode where Hibbert attempts to evade further participation in the forthcoming attack. Stanhope initially threatens to shoot Hibbert - a fate which would have befallen him anyway, had he deserted. Then, when Hibbert breaks down, Stanhope tells him that he is experiencing exactly the same fears himself. In threatening to shoot Hibbert, we can see that Stanhope places the morale and well-being of the whole company above that of any one man, including himself. If Hibbert had been allowed to carry on behaving as he was, his duties would have suffered and the men might be put at risk as a consequence - a chance which Stanhope is not prepared to take. Stanhope is also aware that, by leaving, Hibbert would be placing an unfair burden on the officers left behind. He also knows that in the long run, it will be better for Hibbert to stay and face the enemy than run and never know if his courage would have failed him at the vital moment.

Stanhope reveals his own fears to Hibbert both as a means of shaming the junior officer into staying and also to make him realise that feeling terrified is quite common and is nothing of which to be ashamed. This is an interesting point to note as earlier on, he had been worried that Raleigh's letter home might reveal his own fears and perceived weaknesses. Stanhope, it would seem, is more tolerant and forgiving of other people's defects than of his own. It is also worth noting that Stanhope never reveals Hibbert's actions to anyone, which demonstrates his loyalty to his men.

The news of the planned raid hits Stanhope hard. Initially he offers to take part himself, and then tries to persuade the Colonel that Raleigh is unsuited to the task, which may show that he still feels responsible for his old schoolfriend, or that he is concerned that Raleigh's lack of experience may put the raiding party at unneccesary risk. The Colonel, however, refuses to be swayed - he cannot spare Stanhope, and there really is no-one else who can accompany Osborne. Stanhope is clearly worried at having to send anyone on this mission, which he feels is not worth risking the lives of his men.

When Stanhope and Osborne part, there is an unspoken intensity of feeling between them, which is shown in the glances between them and awkward pauses in their conversation. Stanhope agrees to take care of Osborne's belongings but will not acknowledge the possibility that his friend might not return from the raid. He quite rightly points out that he would be lost without Osborne.

When Osborne is killed, Stanhope is bitter and angry and these are feelings which he takes out on Raleigh, who has returned safely, although this could also be because he knows that Osborne was killed while waiting for Raleigh and perhaps he feels that Raleigh is responsible for Osborne's death. He acknowledges to Raleigh that in losing Osborne, he has lost his best friend and the one person in whom he could confide - he is unsure of how he will be able to continue without his "Uncle" by his side. He attempts to mask his emotions once again, by drinking and laughing with Trotter and Hibbert, but eventually reveals his true feelings in another angry outburst against Raleigh.

When his old schoolfriend is injured Stanhope reverts to his real personality, trying to spare Raleigh the knowledge of his impending death. This is the real Stanhope, as he was before he became damaged by his experiences in the war. He tenderly cares for Raleigh and looks after him to the very end. His status as hero is restored - both to Raleigh and to himself: he has done his duty.

Stanhope has a complex character; a strange entwinement of pre-war reticence and wartime raw emotions. Before the war, Stanhope would have been a man who others respected for his strength, bravery, sportsmanship and gentlemanly behaviour. He feels that all of these qualities are now lost to him and no longer seems to understand his own feelings because they are so foreign to him. It is almost impossible for us, in the 21st century, to understand the emotional, physical and psychological trauma of a conflict like the

First World War, but we must also understand that before the war there was a code of conduct for men of Stanhope's class and background which did not involve showing one's emotions or expressing one's feelings. The character of Stanhope that we see in Journey's End is a microcosm of the impact of the First World War on every aspect of life - everything had changed and nothing would ever be the same again.

Maurice Browne, Producer, with members of the original cast for Journey's End, Savoy Theatre, 21 January 1929.
Image courtesy of The Dartington Hall Trust Archive.
Image copyright: Stage Photo Company.

RALEIGH

Raleigh is the innocent young recruit who arrives, excited at being involved in the war, and particularly at being able to serve under his old schoolboy hero, Stanhope. He is described as a handsome, healthy, but somewhat naive and inexperienced young man.

Upon first arriving, Raleigh is nervous and eager to please, although unsure of how he is supposed to behave. He talks enthusiastically to Osborne of his pre-war friendship with "Dennis" Stanhope. He reveals that he has used his uncle, General Raleigh's, influence to achieve this posting, because he desperately wanted to serve under his old schoolfriend. This is probably partly because Stanhope has always taken care of him and Raleigh hopes this will continue at the front, but also because he simply worships Stanhope and desperately wants to be with him, and follow in his footsteps.

Despite Osborne's friendly warnings about the effect that three years fighting has had on Stanhope, Raleigh is still surprised by Stanhope's appearance and his less than enthusiastic welcome. It is as though Raleigh had expected their relationship to be exactly the same as it was when they were at school. Upon first witnessing Stanhope's drunkenness, Raleigh appears shocked and seems to prefer not to be in company with his old friend, choosing instead to go into his own dugout. This may be because he senses that Stanhope resents his presence, but also could be a symptom of denial - Raleigh simply cannot believe that his old friend could be so badly affected, when everyone at home has always believed him to be coping so well with the war.

Stanhope's reaction to his letter also comes as a blow to Raleigh. He had not anticipated that his letter would need to be censored, presumably because he feels that Stanhope should trust him and he is embarrassed by the prospect of Stanhope reading the contents of his letter. Stanhope misreads Raleigh's reluctance and reacts violently towards him. Raleigh seems to understand the effects of the war on Stanhope, but is still confused, and disappointed by his friend's reaction. In this letter, however, he reveals nothing of Stanhope's changed nature, but remains loyal himself, pointing out instead how hardworking and tireless Stanhope is and that he is an excellent and well-respected officer. He finishes by telling his family of his pride in the knowledge that Stanhope is his friend.

On hearing that he is to help lead the raiding party, Raleigh is nervously enthusiastic. As the hour approaches, his nerves begin to dominate his enthusiasm and it is Osborne, rather than Stanhope, who comforts him. His youth and inexperience are revealed in this scene as he talks nervously to Osborne, trying not to dwell on the raid, refusing to have rum in his coffee and pointing out that he has never smoked a cigar before. This also emphasises the difference in age between the two men, with Raleigh seeming, more than ever, like the schoolboy while Osborne is the wise, kind and inspiring "school teacher".

After the raid, when Osborne is dead, Raleigh is clearly in shock and can barely stand up as he speaks to the Colonel. This new experience has made him understand the horror of the war - something which Stanhope had obviously wanted to spare him for as long as possible. Raleigh needs Stanhope's help and support, but receives neither as Stanhope is incapable of dealing with Raleigh's feelings - he is struggling with his own.

Raleigh's decision to remain in the trenches with the men, rather than join in the dinner demonstrates that he has not fully understood the etiquette of the dugout. Despite the impression that the officers are celebrating, they are for the best part, trying to forget what has happened - to drown their sorrows. In addition, Raleigh had noted in his letter than Stanhope spent a great deal of time with the men in the trenches trying to cheer them up and ease their fears. Perhaps by remaining in the trenches he is trying to emulate his hero - to please him and relieve him of the worry of looking after the men. This backfires as Stanhope is angry with Raleigh for having missed the dinner. He takes it as a personal slight to himself and the other officers. During their argument Raleigh comes to realise how much Osborne had meant to Stanhope. He feels left out of Stanhope's thoughts and doesn't understand his reactions. He wants to be involved and to help Stanhope, but cannot because his friend will not communicate with him. Raleigh would prefer to talk about his feelings, both for Osborne and for Stanhope, but Stanhope rejects this overture, angrily pushing Raleigh away.

Ultimately, the only time that Raleigh is able to recapture the old Stanhope, is on his death-bed, as we get a glimpse of what their relationship once was. His hero looks after him and ensures that he feels safe, comfortable and unafraid.

Overall there is an awkwardness between Raleigh and Stanhope because Raleigh had assumed that by being with Stanhope, everything would be as it had been at school. He has also failed to understand that the war has changed Stanhope to such an extent - he remembers his friend as a young dashing officer, keen to join the fight, and barely recognises the man he has become. Stanhope, on the other hand, resents Raleigh's presence as a reminder of his old life and the person he once was. In addition, Stanhope has formed new friendships now, especially with Osborne, who he looks up to and respects. These are not the sort of feelings he can have for Raleigh whose innocence represents everything he has lost.

Sherriff uses Raleigh's character within the play is to represent Stanhope's past and through Raleigh's descriptions of the pre-war Stanhope, the audience can understand the huge impact that the war could have on an individual. We know that Stanhope has been serving in the war for three years, and can easily imagine him arriving at the front with the same attitude as Raleigh demonstrates. We are then invited to contrast this with the reality of Stanhope as he is now and experience the damage done to him during his three years of service. Raleigh's role also demonstrates the loss of youth, innocence and ultimately life, which was involved in the First World War. Literally within hours of his arrival, he is sent on a raid during which a valued member of the team is killed. This experience changes the young officer, who had been keen to join in the fighting with his old school friend. He no longer views the war as a great adventure. Then during his first few minutes of battle, he is killed, without ever really living.

OSBORNE

While significantly older than Stanhope, Osborne is junior in rank. Married, with two children, he is physically tough and rugged - the opposite of his personality which is level-headed, friendly and trusting. His feelings for his family are clear when he tells Stanhope that he spent the whole of his last leave at home with them, not even going to see any shows. He describes with great warmth the peaceful evenings spent with his wife and playing at soldiers with his two sons. His choice of reading material is interesting: *Alice's Adventures in Wonderland* presumably reminds him of happier times at home with his children. However, once he is back at the front, the Company become his family.

Osborne is very protective of Stanhope, trying to help him wherever possible. Their relationship is not based on hero-worship: Osborne knows and appreciates Stanhope's faults but his respect for his senior officer is borne out of years of experience and time spent with Stanhope at the front. Osborne realises that being in command brings with it heavy responsibilities and he knows that these have taken their toll on Stanhope; despite this, however, Stanhope has remained an excellent and diligent officer, and it is this which earns him Osborne's love and respect. He defends Stanhope's actions to Raleigh and especially Hardy, showing his loyalty to his commanding officer.

Osborne is very kind to Raleigh, who is nervous when he first arrives. He tries to warn Raleigh that Stanhope has changed and also attempts to deflect Raleigh's hero-worship by pointing out that he had played rugby for Harlequins and England. This is not done in a boastful manner, but more as a means of diverting Raleigh's attention from Stanhope, who he knows will be troubled by Raleigh's presence. He is not a vain man which he demonstrates when Hardy suggests that he would make a better Commanding Officer than Stanhope - a suggestion which he adamantly refutes.

As a former schoolmaster, Osborne is used to looking after boys, and his position in the dugout seems to be an extension of this role, to the point where he is nicknamed "Uncle". The use of this name gives Osborne an air of homeliness and reliability, which helps to make the atmosphere in the dugout seem less oppressive. He is always on hand with sensible advice and words of wisdom and is keen to avoid conflict within the dugout. It is always Osborne who helps Stanhope, especially when he is drunk, or over-tired. His first concern is to protect his Commanding Officer from the prying eyes and judgement of others, but also from the most destructive influence in Stanhope's life - himself. Within this role, he takes the decision to read Raleigh's letter to Stanhope, fully understanding that Stanhope must know the contents or he will dwell on what Raleigh might have written. In reading this letter, Osborne's self-effacing nature is demonstrated as he appears embarrassed by Raleigh's praise of him.

Osborne is very diplomatic: for example, his method of getting Mason to wash the dish-cloth is to ask his wife to send him out some soap powder and then suggest to Mason that he might like to try using it. Also when there is obviously a problem with Hibbert, Osborne deflects Trotter's enquiries and changes the subject. When Stanhope suggests that he will deface Trotter's chart of circles by drawing a picture of Trotter being blown up at the time when the attack is anticipated, Osborne dissuades him. This is not because he can really see the point behind Trotter's chart, but because he knows that Trotter had spent a considerable amount of time producing it in the first place and would be offended to have his chart ruined. Maybe, however, unlike Stanhope, Osborne realises that Trotter will see the significance of the drawing and knows that, as such, it will only add to the tension within the dugout. He understands that some of the men need to be able to look on the bright side of things and that Trotter hopes they will survive the attack and go back down the line again, even if Stanhope believes that is impossible.

His reaction upon being told that he is to lead the raid, and his desire not to talk about it beforehand, demonstrate that he is wary of being sent on this mission. He is an officer of some experience and has been on raids before, but now he seems to have a sense of his own mortality as he gives his belongings to Stanhope for safe-keeping, to be returned to his wife should he not survive. He manages to overcome his own fear, at least for appearance's sake, and calms the nerves of Raleigh, who has never experienced anything like this before and, as the hour approaches, becomes more and more nervous.

Osborne's attitude towards the men is always caring and considerate and although he is an officer of some standing, he has not yet become war-weary, like Stanhope. He has a sensible yet realistic perspective of the war and his duty.

Osborne's death signifies a change for this small group of officers. Raleigh, who was with him at the time, feels guilty and disturbed by Osborne's death, while Stanhope has lost the one fellow officer he knew he could trust implicitly. Even if the attack had not happened the next morning, one senses that this Company of men would never have been quite the same again.

The purpose of Osborne's character is to demonstrate the waste of the war and the fact that it is often the most valuable member of a team who will be lost. Although Stanhope is in charge of the Company, it is Osborne who holds them all together and gives the Company its stability. Sherriff is using Osborne to remind the audience that death has no respect for a man's ability or value. In addition, Osborne's death makes the audience wonder how Stanhope will cope without him. We have already witnessed Stanhope's strong dependence on Osborne in every aspect of his position, and his death poses the question of Stanhope's leadership abilities now that he is on his own. Of course, in the end, Stanhope copes well, reverting to his old personality when the need to help Raleigh arises, before going to face his own fate.

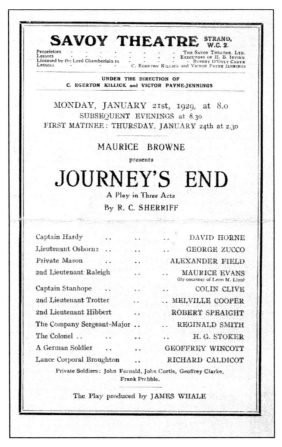

Cast list from the *Journey's End* programme at the Savoy Theatre 1929.
Image courtesy of The Dartington Hall Trust Archive.

TROTTER

Trotter is not in the best physical shape - he is rotund and red-faced. He is also middle-aged with a bursting tunic - the result, no doubt, of too much indulgence in his favourite interest - the consumption of food. He is married and his letters to his wife and descriptions of his home life, such as his garden, serve to remind us that all of these men have something to live for, and so much to lose.

He is a friendly, tolerant character, who is supportive of his fellow officers and loyal to Stanhope. He is also concerned about Stanhope's drinking and health, although he does not have the same close relationship as his Commanding Officer shares with Osborne. His concerns for Stanhope could stem from his fears that if Stanhope becomes too unstable, the Company could be put at risk. Unlike the other officers, Trotter has been promoted through the ranks and, this would give him a better impression of the men's needs with regards to strong leadership. In addition he may be worried that if Stanhope has to be replaced by another officer, the Company will lose its identity as a unit.

Trotter, presumably, does not have the same public school background as the other officers, which is demonstrated by the fact that his language is more colloquial than theirs. Outwardly, Trotter appears to be very unemotional, but the impression is given that this is only on the surface and that Trotter's feelings go much deeper than it would seem. In fact, when Stanhope says that he envies Trotter for being able to maintain a sense of normality, Trotter makes it clear that this is most definitely not the case. He doesn't like to talk about how he feels, using humour to overcome difficult circumstances, and therefore he falsely creates the impression that he doesn't worry about anything - that everything is a joke, but maybe this is just a mask to hide his own fears in the only way he knows.

Stanhope, while liking Trotter, feels that he lacks imagination: he believes that he and Osborne look more deeply at life, while Trotter merely observes what is on the surface. This demonstrates one of the perceived differences between their classes. They have drive and ambition, while Trotter is happy with his lot in life. This is reinforced later on, when he points out that he has never owned a car, but that he and his wife used to walk everywhere together, but he does not seem to resent the fact that others have more than him.

After Osborne's death, Trotter becomes Stanhope's second-in-command, but this brief relationship is more formal than Stanhope and Osborne's had been. Trotter feels honoured by the promotion and promises not to let Stanhope down. He is an honourable and decent man. Even on the final morning, immediately before the dreaded attack, Trotter appears cheerful - he sings songs while in his dugout which helps to relieve the feeling of tension and probably also serves to take his own mind off what might lie ahead.

Some critics describe Trotter as an artificial character - somewhat unnecessary to the plot. This does him a grave injustice as his importance lies in the subtleties of what he says: his reactions demonstrate the common feeling. So, for example, he's worried about the raid - even though he is not involved - but he knows that it is useless to argue, as the orders will not be revoked, no matter how pointless and costly the raid might be. He knows that nothing he can do will change the course of the war, but equally he does not see why he should have to suffer more discomfort than is absolutely necessary. Much of the humour in the play emanates from Trotter and centres on his love of food. Not only does he joke about things, but the others make fun of him, although this is never done offensively, but in friendship.

HIBBERT

Hibbert is a young, slightly obscure man with a pale face - reminiscent of a weasel - both in appearance and manner.

First impressions of Hibbert are not good. He complains of feeling unwell almost continuously and craves escape from the trenches.

Hibbert doesn't initially interact with his fellow-officers, although he knows them all well, having been with them for approximately three months. Instead he prefers to sleep and keep his own company whenever he is not on duty, although one gets the impression that he may be doing this to support his argument that he is unwell.

During his quarrel with Stanhope, it becomes clear that Hibbert is terrified of going back into the trenches and is persuaded to stay only by Stanhope first threatening and then sympathising with him. This exchange shows Hibbert in an unfavourable light and although he agrees to stay, he then becomes concerned that Stanhope might tell the others of his cowardice. This confirms that Stanhope had been right in his assumption that Hibbert was faking his physical illness, and also shows that Hibbert is a shallow man whose sole concerns are his own welfare and reputation, rather than the well-being of the Company as a whole.

This bad impression is exacerbated by his reaction to Osborne's death. Whereas for Trotter and Stanhope, the meal and light conversation are a means to forget, Hibbert uses this opportunity to show off his lewd postcards and boast of his exploits with women - he simply wants to enjoy himself. He also gossips about Raleigh, passing information to Stanhope, which shows he does not share the common sense of loyalty, which he seems to expect of others. Stanhope's distaste for Hibbert is obvious throughout the play, but really comes out in this scene.

When the time comes to go back into the trenches, Hibbert is again hesitant and fearful. In fact he has to be called several times before appearing on the morning of the final attack. He seems unwilling to go up into the trenches, wasting a great deal of time and making excuses, until Stanhope tells him to accompany Mason. This is Stanhope's way of shaming Hibbert into doing his duty - if Mason can do it, so can he. Although this works and Hibbert goes, he hesitates again and, unlike all the others, does not say anything to Stanhope.

Hibbert's role within the play is to remind the audience that not all of the officers were 'decent' or 'gentlemanly'. Hibbert's postcard collection and tales of his adventures with women reinforce this impression. Another purpose of Hibbert's character is to demonstrate Stanhope's belief that the good of the Company must come before the individual. Stanhope's reactions to Hibbert - continually giving him more chances even when he is insubordinate and attempts to hit his Commanding Officer - and his attempts to make Hibbert see sense show his capacity to help others, even if he doesn't particularly like them himself. In addition, the fact that Hibbert is not a very likeable character makes the audience question their own values. One realises that Hibbert's life seems less valuable than Osborne's, for example, but through Stanhope's reactions, Sherriff is making the audience question this viewpoint. In other words, if Stanhope can be bothered to make the effort on behalf of someone like Hibbert, then why shouldn't we?

MASON

Mason is essentially a servant and his general responsibility is to take care of the officers to whom he is assigned. He cooks their meals and clears up after them. This does not, however, mean that he escapes the fighting - he must also take part in any battles in which his company are involved.

Although we are told little about Mason's appearance or personality, we can conclude that he is hard-working, loyal and caring. He never questions his orders, and is keen to please. For example, prior to the final battle, he makes sandwiches for the officers, before going up into the trenches. Mason is often the butt of light-hearted jokes about food and cooking, but this is done without malice.

When Stanhope suggests that Hibbert and Mason go up into the trench together, Mason appears grateful, which may demonstrate his own nervousness. This could, however, be interpreted as showing Mason's understanding of the real situation surrounding Hibbert and his desire to be useful to Stanhope.

The role of Mason's character in the play is to provide humourous respite in the building tension, his interactions with Trotter being particularly amusing. He also serves to remind us that, for the officers in the dugout, in spite of their surroundings and horrific experiences, ordinary activities still go on. The men must eat, and the discussion of what they are eating and how it has been cooked provides a useful diversion from the war, and in many cases, helps to enhance the human qualities of the play.

HARDY

Hardy is a Captain, who commands the company from whom Stanhope's men are taking over. It would seem that he has been at the front for some time, as nothing really seems to surprise him. His role in the play is to set the scene. His conversation with Osborne serves the purpose of explaining the anticipated attack, and Stanhope's personality, as well as some of the boredom and routine of trench-life. We also learn that the opinion of other officers regarding Stanhope's personality is very different from that of his loyal Osborne.

Hardy is a humourous, philosophical character, who has a light-hearted outlook on almost everything, including the general hardships of the war, although this might be more obvious as he is being relieved and going behind the lines - whether he would be as amused if he were the one coming into the trenches is another matter.

This initial scene involving Hardy helps to set the tone for the rest of the play, and helps the reader or audience appreciate that this black humour was an important aspect of life in the trenches. During this scene, as well as learning about the still absent Stanhope, we also learn a great deal about Osborne and how well-respected he is amongst the other men - even those not in his own Company.

HISTORICAL SIGNIFICANCE

The historical setting of the play is significant and accurate. The play starts on March 18th 1918 which was three days before the Germans launched "Operation Michael" at St Quentin.

This was Germany's attempt to end the war before the Americans could arrive in any great number and therefore tip the balance of power in favour of the Allies. Germany, like most of the countries involved in the First World War, was running out of men of military age and the success of this attack was therefore vital.

General Erich Ludendorff declared that the object of this attack must be a resounding victory over the British and the selection of the place for the proposed attack was therefore, of great importance. Immediately in front of the St Quentin trenches was the old Somme battlefield. This was difficult terrain which consisted of water-logged shell-holes and abandoned trenches. Ludendorff thought that, both tactically and psychologically, this was the ideal place to strike. The intention was that, by use of specialist storm troops, the German army would punch a hole in the British front line, and force a retreat towards the coast. However, Ludendorff had no fixed idea as to what would follow this initial strike.

The first days of this battle were extremely bloody and losses on both sides were heavy. It would not be surprising, therefore, if all the characters in *Journey's End* died, since the bombardment and subsequent attack resulted in many British deaths. As a result of these initial losses and the speed of the German advance, the Allied armies became separated which resulted in arguments between Haig (Commander in Chief of the British Army) and Pétain (his equivalent in the French force). At a hastily convened meeting the Allies decided to have one Supreme Commander, which it was decided should be Marshal Ferdinand Foch. This was a significant step and enabled the Allies to fight in a more co-ordinated fashion, with reserves and weaponry being better deployed.

Germany failed to exploit her initial successes and rather than continuing with the plan of a single-pronged attack, her forces became divided. In addition, the selection of the old Somme battleground now seemed unwise as it proved to be difficult terrain for an attacking army to advance over. In addition, the Germans had advanced much further than their lines of supply could support, so by 5th April the German High Command were forced to admit that Operation Michael had achieved as much as could be expected, and further attacks in this area were abandoned.

Before long, American troops began to arrive and this had a great demoralising effect on the German army. Attacks continued at other points on the front and it would take many more months, and many many more deaths before the war was over.

General
Henri-Philippe Pétain

Marshal
Ferdinand Foch

Images courtesy of Photo's of the Great War

The ruins of St Quentin.
Image courtesy of Photo's of the Great War

Entrance to St Quentin canal tunnel under the ridge at Bellicourt, on the Hindenburg Line.
Image courtesy of Photo's of the Great War

PORTRAYAL OF THE RANKS IN THE BRITISH ARMY

Some students find the named ranks and their responsibilities difficult to interpret. The following provides a very brief outline of the role of each of the ranks involved in *Journey's End*, together with an explanation of Sherriff's use and portrayal of these ranks.

COLONEL

The most senior officer involved in the play, the Colonel is, in all probability, in charge of a battalion of over 1000 men, divided into four companies. The company involved in *Journey's End* is 'C' Company. During the course of the war, with the influx of the New Armies and the number of casualties the quantity of men in a battalion varied widely.

In the case of *Journey's End*, the Colonel is portrayed as someone who only visits the dugout when absolutely necessary, and then only to send valuable and inexperienced men on pointless missions, while inviting Stanhope to join him for a dinner of fresh fish. Whether this portrayal was entirely intentional on Sherriff's part, is a matter of conjecture. However, many modern historians, especially those with a military background, would disagree with this heartless depiction, pointing out that if the senior officers spent all their time in the trenches, there would have been no-one left to control the overall direction of the war. Others, with more 'cultural' or 'social' agenda would argue that the senior officers were controlling the war from too great a distance, with too many perks and advantages when compared to those at the front line. Sherriff's portrayal of the Colonel would seem to indicate that he sided with the latter viewpoint, although this may be based only on his own experiences of senior officers with whom he personally came into contact. The Colonel in Journey's End is given few redeeming qualities. Before the raid, he speaks in a very matter-of-fact way about sending men to their possible deaths. Afterwards, he barely remembers to ask about the fate of those who went on the mission.

However, although the Colonel may seem outwardly enthusiastic, offering gushing encouragement to Raleigh and Osborne, his hesitations and embarrassed coughs show that he is also aware of the magnitude of the task at hand. One of Sherriff's reasons behind writing the play was to demonstrate the willingness of men to do their duty. The Colonel is, therefore, doing his duty, in the same way as Stanhope and all the others. He takes his orders from Brigade Headquarters and regardless of his own viewpoint, must see to it that these orders are carried out.

CAPTAIN

This rank belongs to the characters of both Stanhope and Hardy. These men are both in charge of companies of approximately 230 men. They are responsible for the maintenance of their area of trench, as well as the morale and physical well-being of the men under their command. It is their duty to ensure that the men are in a fit state to undertake whatever tasks they must perform - whether that involves fighting in battle or 'fatigues' (manual labour, such as clearing roads, digging trenches etc.)

Sherriff's portrayal of the men in this role shows that he seems to have held them in higher esteem than their superiors. This might seem hardly surprising, since this was the rank achieved by Sherriff himself! However, he was not alone in this opinion. A look at Undertones of War by Edmund Blunden for example, reveals a similar perspective. This memoir and Sherriff's play were both published at around the same time, and the two writers were, to a greater or lesser extent, haunted by their wartime experiences and sought to commemorate, or celebrate the comradeship and honour they had discovered during their First World War service.

In *Journey's End*, Stanhope is shown to be the man who bears all the responsibility for his men, and their well-being, while remaining extremely critical and self-effacing about his own abilities and qualities. By showing us an imperfect man, who survives on the edge, Sherriff enhances the audience's sense of sympathy for this central character. The cheerfulness of Hardy, the other Captain in the play, contrasts well with Stanhope's more troubled personality, although one should always remember that it is easier for Hardy to be cheerful as he is being relieved and going back down the line, further away from the impending attack.

LIEUTENANTS AND SECOND LIEUTENANTS

These ranks apply to all the other officers in the play. It may fairly be assumed that Osborne is superior in rank to Trotter, Hibbert and Raleigh, as he is Stanhope's second-in-command, so he probably holds the rank of Lieutenant, while the others are Second-Lieutenants. Their responsibilities were essentially to help their captain in maintaining the day-to-day running of the company. In addition, each of these men would have been responsible for a Platoon within the company, consisting of approximately 50 men each.

Sherriff portrays the few men who hold these ranks as having realistically diverse characters - from the strong, reliable Osborne, to the unpleasant, cowardly Hibbert. This reminds the audience that men from many different walks of life found themselves serving together during the First World War. There was an unprecedented mixing of classes and backgrounds in the war, which is ably depicted in the characters of Raleigh and Trotter. Raleigh is portrayed as a naive public schoolboy who has, until now, led a sheltered life, protected by his friend Stanhope, and using his family's substantial influence to achieve his ambitions. Trotter, on the other hand, would seem to be from a lower social class than Raleigh and he has been promoted through the ranks. This type of officer often found himself in a difficult position, as he did not really fit in with the 'gentleman' officers, but was equally out of place among the ordinary soldiers. While Trotter gets on quite well with all the other officers in the dugout, there is a sense of isolation within his character which may stem from a belief that he is different from them.

COMPANY SERGEANT-MAJOR

This rank is held by the most senior non-commissioned officer in a company. A commissioned officer being one who has been charged, or 'commissioned' into a specific position. The CSM is, generally speaking, responsible for standards and discipline amongst the lower ranks. Beneath him there would be other sergeants and the men. In times of battle the CSM is responsible for seeing to the safe removal of the wounded and dealing with prisoners

The CSM in *Journey's End* is an accurate representation of this rank. He oversees the German prisoner, and it is he who reports Raleigh's injuries to Stanhope and brings the wounded man into the dugout. In addition the CSM's role within the play is to remind us of the men who are out in the trenches. Being as the action takes place entirely in the dugout, the audience could easily forget the existence of anyone else without the link provided by the CSM.

Stanhope's briefing of the CSM prior to the attack also serves to further demonstrate Stanhope's character. Despite the CSM's concerns that they should have a plan for withdrawal if the enemy should overpower them, Stanhope refutes this idea. Instead, he suggests that the Company should advance, rather than retreat and should keep going until they have won the war! Stanhope is not being naive here, he is pointing out to the CSM, an experienced man himself, that they must hold their position because others are relying on them.

OTHER RANKS

These include Sergeants, Corporals, Lance Corporals and Privates. The only named 'other rank' in the play is Mason, the officer's servant, who in this role would be the only soldier, other than the officers, to spend much time in the dugout.

Although Mason is the only ranking soldier of whom we see a great deal, Sherriff portrays the unseen men as worthy of respect. Stanhope is always shown as being concerned for their welfare, checking that they have had their allocation of rum and refusing to allow an officer from another company to take part in the raid in case it damages the men's morale. Like much else in this play, this is also done to reinforce Stanhope's character. We have been told right at the beginning that Hardy had no idea where his men slept, yet Raleigh's letter demonstrates that Stanhope spends a lot of time with his men, taking great care of them.

HE NEW YORK TIMES, TUESDAY, NOVEMBER 18, 1975

R. C. Sherriff, Playwright, Dies; Author of 'Journey's End Was 79

His World War I Tragicomedy Gained Wide Recognition as Anti-War Classic

LONDON (AP)—Robert C. Sherriff, who wrote the play "Journey's End" about World War I, died on Thursday. He was 79 years old.

Based on Mr. Sherriff's three years' service in the war, "Journey's End" was first produced in 1928 and ran for 594 performances in London. A film version was made in English and German.

Stage productions eventually appeared in 20 countries.

Mr. Sherriff also was a novelist. He went to Hollywood in the 1930's and became literary adviser to Alexander Korda. He wrote screenplays for the films "The Invisible Man" (1933), "Goodbye, Mr. Chips" (1936) and "The Dam Busters" (1955).

R. C. Sherriff

Interested in Dramatics

Mr. Sheriff was an insurance man interested in amateur dramatics who was active in the Kingston-on-Thames Rowing Club. He turned out a play the club could perform with an all-male cast, based on his introduction to combat at Vimy Ridge in World War I. To a newly arrived second lieutenant aged 20, the camaraderie and strain among the officers of Company C, Ninth Battalion, East Surrey Regiment, made a lasting impression. The play was a cross-section of the comedy and tragedy of trench life on the edge of death for men who were not quite sure what it was all about.

When the club felt inadequate to take it on, he offered it to professional producers, who turned it down. The actor Leslie Banks took it to the Incorporated Stage Society of London, which gave it a single performance on Dec. 9, 1928. The cast was headed by an unknown from the Birmingham Repertory Company named Laurence Olivier. Others in the cast were Melville Cooper and Maurice Evans.

Success Then Spread

The playwright Maurice Browne bought the rights and took the production to the Savoy Theater where is opened Jan. 21, 1929. Its success was soon echoed in Paris, Berlin and New York, where it opened on March 22 and ran for more than a year while four touring companies took it on the road all over the country. In theater terms the play's deglamorization of war caught on with the public in many countries, in somewhat the same vein as Ernest Hemingway's "A Farewell to Arms" and Erich Maria Remarque's "All Quiet on the Western Front."

The play stood the test of a 1972 revival in London, where The Guardian called it "a fascinating document of war."

Although Mr. Sherriff was able to make a career of writing after that with a series of novels, plays, and screenplays, many of them displaying manly virtue in the stiff-upper-lip tradition, nothing quite matched his first success.

R C Sherriff obituary from The New York Times, Tuesday November 18th 1975. *Image courtesy of The Dartington Hall Trust Archive.*

R C SHERRIFF - BIOGRAPHICAL DETAIL

Robert Cedric Sherriff was born on 6th June 1896 in Kingston-upon-Thames, although some sources say he was born in adjacent Hampton Wick. He was educated at Kingston Grammar School and then New College, Oxford. He worked in his father's insurance company until the outbreak of the First World War.

In August 1914, Sherriff attempted to obtain a commission into the British Army. He later related the story of his interview with an adjutant, presumably with some irony. Sherriff, it would seem, was informed that he would probably not be a suitable candidate for a commission as he had not attended a public school. Somewhat mystified by this, he explained that his school was a good one and had been founded by Queen Elizabeth I in 1567. However, the adjutant remained unimpressed - pointing out that his orders were only to accept applications from men who had attended recognised public schools.

The stupidity of this ruling must have had a bearing on Sherriff, who despite his supposedly "poor" education was no less qualified to serve as an officer than his public school colleagues.

Sherriff went on to serve as a captain in the East Surrey Regiment, arriving in France on 28th September 1916. After the war, he rejoined his father's company, where he remained for the next ten years.

He had always been interested in amateur theatricals and wrote plays for performance by members of the Kingston Rowing Club to raise money for a new boat. This led him to write *Journey's End*, based on his experiences in the war. The play was first performed one Sunday evening in December 1928 and went on to become a huge success.

This achievement enabled Sherriff to become a full-time writer and he went on to write many more plays and several screen plays for films including *Goodbye Mr Chips*, *The Four Feathers* and *The Dam Busters*. He also published his autobiography, No Leading Lady, in 1968.

He lived in Esher, Surrey until his death on 13th November 1975. He left his house, named Rosebriars to Elmbridge Borough Council for social and cultural purposes. The capital raised from the sale of this house established the R C Sherriff Rosebriars Trust which still exists today to promote the arts in the Borough of Elmbridge.

THEMES

FUTILITY AND WASTE

Journey's End is now generally recognised as an anti-war play, although some historians doubt that this was Sherriff's original intention. Some confusion, it would seem, arose from a difference of opinion between Sherriff and the play's original producer. Sherriff's intention was, rather, to portray the pride which the men felt in each other and the comradeships which developed in such difficult circumstances. In doing so, he also demonstrates the inescapable human cost of the war. The men seem to be required to make great sacrifices and it is made clear that even those who survived would never be the same again. Death is indiscriminate, taking those who least deserve to fall, and these deaths are seen to serve little or no purpose. Any gains made are certainly not worth the loss of such valued characters. The men are generally portrayed as worthy people who have accepted their presence in the war as a duty they have to perform - a necessary evil. Although the men, especially Stanhope, may question the value of activities such as the raid, none of them speak out against the war itself, despite the fact that it costs them all dearly.

These themes are best demonstrated immediately before and after the raid, led by Osborne and Raleigh. The purpose of this raid is to capture some German soldiers to find out where the anticipated attack is likely to take place, and the strength and nature of the opposing army. The colonel points out, somewhat optimistically, that the success of this raid may constitute an Allied victory. However, the discovery of the type of opposition you are facing is unlikely to affect the outcome of a battle, if you have nothing more to throw at it yourself. Therefore, it would seem that the colonel is seeking to justify the raid, when in fact, as Stanhope suggests, there can be no justification for such a waste of lives. The raiding party manages to capture a young German soldier, whose limited information is greeted with disproportionate pleasure by the Colonel. He appears to feel that the raid has accomplished its aims. The details given by the captured German soldier, however, seem insignificant compared with the loss of life necessitated during his seizure.

The deaths of Osborne and six of the men accompanying him, is a great price for this Company to pay. For Osborne - surely the most likeable character in the play - to have died at all is lamentable, but to have died for so little and in such circumstances is tragic - a point which Stanhope grasps, and which makes him bitter and angry towards the Colonel. Stanhope appreciates that it is really Osborne who holds the Company together, not himself, because he has come to rely so heavily on Osborne as the war has progressed. Nothing has really been gained by these deaths and Sherriff uses Osborne's death in particular to reinforce the idea of this war's wanton destruction of the best men of his generation.

Throughout the play, however, Sherriff also shows that death is not the only means of wasting a life: Stanhope has virtually suffered a nervous breakdown, changing from the self-assured, sportsman and hero of Raleigh's description, to a confused and moody wreck, who doubts his own abilities and constantly looks to Osborne for reassurance. Raleigh, on the other hand, loses his innocence: he learns a difficult lesson as he comes to realise that Stanhope is not the man he once knew and that the war has changed his friend forever. Ultimately Raleigh also loses his life - within a few minutes of his first experience of battle - but not before he has witnessed the physical and emotional damage that the war can bring about. Had either Stanhope or Raleigh lived, it is unlikely that they would ever have fully recovered from their experiences. Stanhope actually realises this already, as he shows in his conversation with Osborne, when he says that if he survives he will go away by himself for a long time, to recover his health, before trying to face Madge again.

Another example of futility comes in a seemingly strange conversation when Osborne and Stanhope discuss the fate of worms. The two men agree that worms probably have no idea in which direction they are travelling and how rotten and confusing this must be for them. This minor conversation could be interpreted as a reference to the equal pointlessness of the men's existence - they also have very little idea of where they are going, or why, and yet as Osborne says - with more than an air of sarcasm, this pointlessness and confusion is dreaded by the worms more than anything else. He is implying that there are worse situations to be in than wasting your time drifting aimlessly; being killed, without ever really understanding the reason, for example, could as easily befall the worm or the soldier.

The choice of *Alice's Adventures in Wonderland* as reading material for Osborne is also interesting. Osborne quotes from the book to Trotter, who finds the passage pointless and playfully mocks Osborne for reading a children's book. Of course, Osborne's point is that it *is* pointless - not just the passage quoted, but everything - this story represents how little meaning there is in the men's lives, and how nonsensical the whole war has become. For most of the men, especially those like Stanhope and Raleigh, the point of joining up was for the "adventure" and to do their duty, not to sit around in trenches, waiting to be blown up, or being sent on pointless raids into No Man's Land.

BOREDOM AND TENSION

Most of the play is spent waiting for something to happen, whether it is a raid, the impending attack or the serving of a meal. Hardy tells us right at the beginning of the play that the men can sit in boredom for hours and hours and then, suddenly, without warning, something unexpected will happen.

The tension created by this sense of anticipation provokes different responses in each of the characters. Hibbert, for example, dreads going up into the trenches and longs for the waiting to continue - anything as long as he doesn't have to face the realities of his situation. He spends most of his time asleep in his dugout, not mixing with the other men. By avoiding them he also avoids the issue of what might be about to happen, because he is not there to hear it being discussed. His supposed illness is his means of trying to escape, although it also tells us a lot about his personality. Hibbert's reaction is a form of denial: by pretending to be unwell and avoiding the others, he is trying to appear as though the war has not really affected him psychologically, but that it has made him physically ill. The truth, of course, is revealed during his argument with Stanhope, when he is forced to confess his real feelings.

Stanhope on the other hand, 'copes' by keeping busy, not sleeping and drinking himself into oblivion. By doing this he not only takes his mind off the reality of his life, but also helps to pass the time doing anything other than thinking - a necessity of his position which has become abhorrent to him. In addition to not thinking about his current situation any more than is absolutely necessary, Stanhope also seems to have been avoiding thoughts of his past. Raleigh's arrival necessities a resurgence of these memories and, for the first time, he tells Osborne about his feelings for Madge. Osborne is Stanhope's closest friend and yet he has never spoken of Raleigh's sister before. He has obviously found it necessary to block out his memories of the past, in order to maintain a semblance of a focus on the present. Remembering these things only seems to add to his tensions which become more obvious as the raid approaches. He paces the floor, glances about anxiously, checks his watch repeatedly - showing that the strain of waiting is making him even more nervous than normal. He also busies himself with the last-minute preparations so as to avoid thinking about what might happen.

Osborne tries to help wherever he can and relieves his boredom by reading *Alice's Adventures in Wonderland*. He is a great observer of everything which is happening around him. He talks to the others, helping to relieve their nerves, especially Raleigh, who has no idea what to expect. Probably the most tense moment in the play is the scene between Raleigh and Osborne immediately prior to the raid. Once they have finalised their plans, Osborne suggests that they try to forget about the raid for the final few minutes before it commences. It takes several attempts and a quotation from *Alice in Wonderland* before Osborne succeeds in changing the subject. The tension actually seems to increase as they discuss their homes and talk of Osborne visiting Raleigh after the war. There is an unspoken fear that, in all probability, one or other of these men may not return and they make plans for the future to cover this up.

Trotter eats, thinks about eating, or talks about eating, and writes to his wife of mundane, everyday matters, such as his garden and the lice which have infested his clothing. He has created a chart of circles to count down the hours until they can be relieved and go back down the line. Trotter uses humour to overcome these difficult situations, although there is always the underlying hint that he feels much more than he expresses.

Only Raleigh, the new recruit is, as yet, unaffected by the boredom, as he is keen to impress the others and everything is a new experience for him, so he pays attention and makes sure that he is doing his duty to the best of his ability. Although he is unaware of what lies ahead in the raid, the tension of waiting to go out into No Man's Land is obvious and his nerves start to get the better of his excitement, although Osborne helps to calm him down. Once Osborne has been killed, Raleigh's sense of adventure and excited anticipation disappear, to be replaced by the same sense of sorrow and foreboding as the rest of the men.

In reality these feelings of boredom and tension were common among serving soldiers in the First World War. Much of a soldier's time was spent carrying out fatigues, waiting behind the lines in reserve to be called back to the front. The pent up anticipation and fear which accumulated as they waited for the inevitable attack is admirably captured in this play. The feelings of terror during battles could be said to have been increased by the fact that so much of their time was spent doing mundane and repetitive tasks, waiting for something to happen. It was all or nothing.

SCHOOLDAYS AND HEROES

There is a strong link in this play between life in the trenches and at a "public" school. Not only were Raleigh and Stanhope at the same school, but Osborne, in private life, was a schoolmaster. At the time of the First World War, the title "public" school was given to fee-paying establishments, of which many were also boarding schools. There is an atmosphere of the school dormitory in the dugout, and a definite sense of hierarchy, with certain officers taking precedence over others, and the emphasis being on experience and seniority. For instance, right at the beginning of the play, Hardy points out the best bed in the dugout to Osborne, telling him that the others do not have bottoms to them. As the senior officer of his Company, Hardy has the best bed, while the other officers have to make do with whatever is left. Interestingly though, Stanhope designates the best bed to Osborne, preferring to sleep nearer to the table, so he can work during the night without disturbing anyone else.

Stanhope is given the air of the "head boy", looking after those younger or less experienced than himself, especially the new boy - Raleigh. Although we are led to believe that Stanhope was happy to wear this mantle while at school, it does not sit so well with him now. He says that he used to enjoy looking after Raleigh and the influence that he was able to exert over the younger boy, but now he feels uncomfortable at having so much additional responsibility thrust upon him. He also wishes that he could have been spared the indignity of having Raleigh witness what has become of him - he feels that his hero's crown has slipped and does not want to crush Raleigh's image of him. It would seem that Stanhope took his status at school quite seriously. Raleigh recalls Stanhope's attitude towards smoking and drinking when they were at school, which goes to show how much of an impact the war has had, being as Stanhope now drinks so much himself.

Raleigh, on the other hand, as the new boy is eager to please and do well, just as he probably would have been at school. His personality makes him keen to learn, although he is as yet unsure of the rules and protocols which exist in the trenches. At school, Raleigh had worshiped Stanhope and looked up to him as someone worthy of respect, finding it impossible to see a fault in Stanhope's personality. He is keen that this relationship should continue in the trenches and hopes that Stanhope will not object to his presence. Osborne has to try and warn Raleigh about his hero's altered personality and the effect that the war has had on him. Raleigh's hopes for a resumption of his friendship with Stanhope may be because he assumes that the continuation of certain aspects of his life at home will give him an increased sense of security - reminding him, perhaps, of happier days at school.

Osborne, with his worldly experience is the voice of reason and sanity - the housemaster. He offers sensible advice and provides a caring, responsible figure for the others to turn to. As a former schoolmaster, himself he is perfectly suited to this role as he understands the problems of boys who find themselves away from home, thrust into unfamiliar territory. It must be remembered that Stanhope, when he first went out to the front, and Raleigh, when he arrives, are extremely young - and have arrived straight from school. Osborne's presence must be very welcome and reassuring to both of them, especially given Stanhope's instability. A good example of this relationship is when Stanhope asks Osborne to tuck him up in bed - this shows not only Stanhope's youth, but also Osborne's caring and understanding nature.

We also have Mason, who in the role of servant, helps recreate the public school hierarchy. Many of the boys in a public school at that time would have been accustomed to having servants at home, and within the school itself, younger boys were often expected to fetch and carry (or 'fag') for the more senior pupils. The officers chastise

Mason for not bringing any pepper to go with their soup, and he worries (quite disproportionately) about the prospect of having to serve apricots instead of the desired pineapple. His worries serve to remind us of his 'inferior' status, when compared to the officers and also of how important mundane matters, such as food, have become to the men.

Trotter is the only one of the officers who, it would seem, did not attend a public school. This is demonstrated by his tone and language, which is more colloquial than the others. Also, we learn that he has risen from the ranks which is interesting, as it means that rather than being commissioned as an officer from the very beginning, he has worked his way up, by being good at what he does. The difference in his education could provide a reason why Trotter keeps his views to himself most of the time: although they are all friendly enough, he possibly does not feel that he really fits in with the others.

Stanhope's treatment of Hibbert, when the latter tries to evade his duties, is equally reminiscent of schooldays. Although he is obviously more extreme in his language and the nature of his threats, one can easily imagine Stanhope berating Hibbert for refusing to turn out for a rugby match, or not doing his best in the last game of cricket. Hibbert is, in fact, the only member of the company who does not show Stanhope very much respect, but then we are not told what his background is, so we do not know whether he was a public schoolboy. His language ties in with most of the other officers, but his behaviour is not so honourable as theirs. It is possible, therefore, that Hibbert's education was of a 'grammar school' nature. Grammar schools at this time would have also been fee-paying, but the charges would have been much smaller than those of 'public' schools and provided a sound education. Hibbert's less than appealing character could be the result of his belief that he has had less opportunities in life than his public school comrades, for whom he may have harboured some resentment.

Within the play there are also many references to rugby and cricket which help reinforce this 'public school' image of England as it was before the First World War when those sports would have been standard and duty and loyalty to the team and one's friends would have been implicit. To be chosen to play for the team was an honour, although such a selection also had the effect of creating heroes, since those chosen were often lauded by their contemporaries, in the same way as top footballers are today.

FAMILY

Whilst these men are all very different, in terms of background, experience and personality, they have become like a family and have adopted roles within that family. There is a powerful sense of belonging and of loyalty which most of the men exhibit throughout the play and those who do not are chastised for their attitude.

Osborne, the oldest and wisest, is nicknamed "Uncle" - a well deserved and appropriate epithet since he is always on hand with sensible advice, is supremely loyal and kind, yet not overbearing or interfering. His maturity and experience, both before and during the war, help him to understand the others. Osborne's adoption of this nickname enhances this family theme and encourages the audience or reader to look for further examples of it.

Stanhope, despite his youth, is a father-figure to his men - which was not an uncommon role for company commanders in the First World War. He has to take all the tough decisions and deal with the consequences both of his own and others' actions. This responsibility weighs heavily on one so young, and has taken its toll on Stanhope, who is on the verge of a nervous breakdown relying heavily on the senior members of his "family" for support. Their loyalty and respect for him are obvious - and well deserved. Despite his many faults, he always puts them first.

Raleigh is the equivalent of the youngest son in the family - looking to his elders for advice and approval. He worships Stanhope blindly and his attachment to his friend is clear: when writing to his family at home, he makes no mention of Stanhope's problems with alcohol or his changed temperament - putting any noticeable changes in Stanhope's personality down to tiredness and overwork. Like many younger sons, he doesn't yet have a fixed idea of what his future holds and is content, for the time being, at least, to follow in the footsteps of those who have preceded him.

The role of older brother goes to Trotter, who is quiet, considerate and has a good sense of humour which sees the family through difficult times. He keeps his own counsel and doesn't interfere but is willing to help when asked. Again, he is loyal to Stanhope, but in a less obvious, more considered manner. He is not blind to Stanhope's faults, but understands their cause and his age and experience allow him to be more tolerant of his surroundings and of the behaviour of others.

Hibbert is the "Black Sheep" of the family, and he sometimes embarrasses those around him by his comments and outbursts. He is the only selfish member of the "family", and his loyalties lie entirely with himself. He shows little or no respect for Stanhope or his fellow officers and his main concern is how to avoid any further involvement in the war.

Mason, in his role as cook, is the equivalent of the household servant, tending to the needs of the family. His loyalty is to all of them, but he answers mainly to Stanhope, who is perceived as the head of the house.

HUMOUR

There is a very effective use of humour, usually of a 'gallows' style, throughout the play.

Very early on, during Hardy's conversation with Osborne, the use of humour demonstrates the need for relief from the everyday horrors of war. The number of rats, the condition of the dugout and beds, the poor storage of ammunition, all of which are very important, are treated in a flippant, lighthearted manner. Other matters, too are treated in the same way, for example the lack of pepper to go with the officer's soup brings a wry comment from Trotter, whose interest in food provides the source of several other jokes. The fact that important and insignificant issues are treated in the same manner shows that, even things which in peacetime might seem unimportant, can, at times of extreme stress, take on a completely different emphasis.

Much of the humour in the play centres around Mason, the cook/servant. His witty responses regarding his cooking, the quality of the food that he is supplying or his standards of hygiene give the play a more homely quality and help to relieve the continually building tension. It should be born in mind that the original audience of the play would have been aware of the significance of the dates during which the action takes place and would have understood the consequences of setting the play at this time. It would have been essential for the author to lighten and relieve the audience's perception of the situation in which the men found themselves. An audience must be entertained as well as enlightened, otherwise the play could never hope to succeed.

This use of humour also helps define the surroundings and the men's state of mind. This could probably have been achieved without the humour, but it would have been less effective. The realistic use of humour makes the whole situation more human, which in turn draws the audience into the world of these men, forcing us to care even more about their survival. We can also appreciate their capacity, through humour, to triumph in the face of adversity - to not give in to their fears and apprehensions, but to rise above them.

Sherriff's use of humour is, at times, more subtle - for example near the end of the play, just before the attack, when Trotter is singing in his dugout, Stanhope throws him a few coins, as though he were a street performer, and Trotter replies in kind. This humour helps in the creation of the atmosphere of camaraderie which is what has kept the men going in the dugout. This is reflected in many of the memoirs written by soldiers who served during the First World War. Without being able to crack a joke, or have a laugh, the tension would have been almost unbearable.

COMPARISONS

Within the realms of formal studies, it is often required of students that they compare and contrast one piece of literature with another, which naturally requires a far greater level of understanding of both pieces and can also necessitate wider reading. Making such comparisons is good practice for students, forcing them into the habit of reading as widely as possible, from as many different sources as are available. This helps with the interpretation and understanding of literature, as well as enabling the student to have a broader perspective of the time during which a piece was written, and how this can influence the writing. The following provides a series of topics contained in *Journey's End* which could be compared or contrasted with other literature of the First World War, including other plays, novels and poems.

MALE RELATIONSHIPS

The first important point to note, within this topic, is the time of publication. *Journey's End* was first published in 1929, which would have made an openly homosexual relationship between two characters impossible, being as homosexuality was, at that time, illegal. This also applies to other books published at that time, such as Remarque's *All Quiet on the Western Front* (1929) and Rebecca West's *The Return of the Soldier* (1918). Novels which have been published in the second half of the twentieth century such as Susan Hill's *Strange Meeting* (1971), Pat Barker's *Regeneration* (1991) and Sebastian Faulks' *Birdsong* (1993) do not have this restriction and the modern authors are therefore able to be more explicit in their content and language, if they choose. However, this difference in the date of publication does not necessarily mean that the more modern authors always refer to this type of relationship between their male characters.

In *Journey's End* the main relationship explored by students is usually that between Stanhope and Raleigh. Stanhope is the senior officer and Raleigh is the new recruit, determined to do well. These two men knew each other before the war and, in fact, Stanhope has "an understanding" with Raleigh's sister. They attended the same school and, Stanhope being good at sport, became an object of hero-worship to Raleigh, and probably many of the other boys at school, even before the war. This has been enhanced by his long service in the trenches, the award of an MC and his command of a Company. Raleigh's feelings for Stanhope could be said to border on a schoolboy "crush", although that is open to interpretation and his somewhat gushing descriptions of Stanhope could be put down to his youthful enthusiasm. He clearly looks up to his friend, while Stanhope feels under great pressure to protect the younger man - an almost impossible task, given their current surroundings. Stanhope's reactions to Raleigh are also tempered by his fear that Raleigh will inform his family, and therefore his sister, of the effect that the war has had on Stanhope's personality. The impression created is that Stanhope has always been popular with Raleigh's family and he is terrified of losing their respect. He has, in fact, managed to avoid seeing either his or Raleigh's family for some time - he would prefer them all to remember him how he was and he can cope better knowing that they continue to believe in him. There is no hint of homosexual love between these two men - in fact Raleigh seems to feel quite honoured that there is a budding romance between his sister and Stanhope.

Sherriff uses the relationship between Stanhope and Raleigh for many purposes: to demonstrate the destructive nature of the war on a man's personality; to highlight the loss of innocence in many young men as a result of their experiences in the trenches; to show the audience how a 'flawed' character like Stanhope can still inspire hero-worship, despite his perceived faults. Raleigh never really loses his faith in Stanhope, and eventually rewarded on his death-bed with a glimpse of his old hero.

Another equally important relationship in *Journey's End* is the one between Stanhope and Osborne. Here, although he is the junior officer, it is really Osborne who is portrayed as the stronger character of the two. His knowledge and understanding of Stanhope enable him to sympathise with his Commanding Officer. He still does his duty while protecting Stanhope from his own self-destruction. Stanhope is occasionally portrayed as almost childlike, which gives his relationship with Osborne a father-and-son perspective. If anything, one feels that the roles should be reversed and that Osborne should be in charge - but like much else in this portrayal of the war - things are not always as they should be. Osborne unashamedly declares his love for Stanhope right at the beginning of the play, but the audience is under no misapprehension that this is a romantic love. He is stating a depth of feeling which shows how much Stanhope means to him - he would willingly follow Stanhope to Hell - but this is due to Osborne's unlimited respect for him, coupled with a mutual understanding and compassion. Sherriff's portrayal of this relationship helps to demonstrate Stanhope's comparative youth and contrasts it with the responsibilities he now has to bear. In addition, Sherriff makes the audience compare this relationship with Stanhope's treatment of Raleigh.

Within this theme, the relationship between Siegfried Sassoon and Wilfred Owen as portrayed in Pat Barker's *Regeneration*, bears some scrutiny. This can, however, be complicated by the fact that there also existed a real-life friendship between them and that *Regeneration* is the first part of a trilogy, so their story is, at the end of this novel, incomplete. Owen hero-worships Sassoon - after all he has shown himself to be a courageous officer, renowned for his daring exploits at the front and is, of course, a published poet - something of which Owen, at this stage, can only dream. Like Raleigh, Owen is always prepared to excuse any sign of rudeness or bad behaviour in his hero, and his feelings within the relationship are by far the stronger. Like Stanhope in *Journey's End*, Sassoon is the older man and is much more experienced - not only as an officer, but also a poet. He wants to guide Owen's poetry and assist him with its publication. Again, though, there is no obvious symptom of romantic love displayed between Owen and Sassoon, although in the novel, Sassoon is seen to doubt this, based on the content and style of Owen's subsequent letters. The relationship between these two poets is also explored in the play *Not About Heroes* by Stephen MacDonald, told from Sassoon's perspective fourteen years after Owen's death.

Another male relationship which is explored in *Regeneration* is that between Billy Prior and Dr Rivers. Like the relationship between Osborne and Stanhope, this is more of a 'father-and-son' situation, but there any similarities end. Billy initially resents Prior's interrogation of him and is abusive towards the doctor, until he eventually realises that Rivers is the only person he can really trust. Rivers understands Billy's troubled personality and wants to protect him even though this must be done at a substantial personal cost to himself. Billy has managed to penetrate Rivers' professional persona and, despite his concerns about this, Rivers allows their strange relationship to continue. Pat Barker's use of this relationship provides a good contrast within the novel with the friendship between Sassoon and Dr Rivers, which is shown to be much deeper and more considered.

A different perspective of a close male relationship can be seen in Susan Hill's novel *Strange Meeting*. The two main characters in this story, Barton and Hilliard, fall deeply in love. There is no evidence that their love is necessarily physical, but that does not make it any less intense and meaningful - if anything the opposite is the case. Although the reader is never made aware of the full nature of their relationship, it is, in fact, irrelevant to the story. Hilliard comes from a background devoid of affection and, finding this in Barton and his family, he is able, for the first time in his life, to experience love. There is not really an element of hero-worship between Barton and Hilliard, although the latter is slightly older and far more experienced. The portrayal of this relationship demonstrates the strength of love as an emotion: it can overcome everything - even the death of one of the parties involved and those touched by it can grow, gaining strength of character and understanding of others.

In *Regeneration* and *Strange Meeting*, the authors are free to be much more explicit about homosexual relationships. This was not a freedom which R C Sherriff would have been able to enjoy. It is unlikely that his play would have been performed had the content appeared homosexual. People at that time were still keen to ensure that the love that had existed between men during the war was "the right kind of love".

The poem *Comrades: An Episode* by Robert Nichols is a very good example of the love and respect which was often felt between officers and men in general, rather than a specific relationship between two men. It also demonstrates how this type of emotion came to have a greater significance, even than familial or romantic ties, due to the mens' shared experiences. Gates, the officer in this poem, lies wounded and dying in No-Man's-Land. Knowing that his life will shortly end, he decides that he must return to his men before he dies. This shows the admiration which he feels for them as well as his dependency on them - he literally decides that he *cannot* face death without seeing his men one last time. Two of his men are shot and killed trying to help him get back into the trench and by the end he bitterly regrets the cost of his decision to return.

To the men, however, it would seem to have been an honour to give their lives for Gates. He was their officer and a man whom they held in the highest esteem. To read this poem helps the modern student understand the strength of emotion between men during the war, in a way that very few pieces achieve.

The way in which the war affects these relationships varies. In *Strange Meeting*, without the war, there may not have been a relationship in the first place. Barton and Hilliard come from very different backgrounds and meet for the first time at the front. In fact, the whole of their time together is spent there. They know that they might die at any moment and this serves to intensify their feelings for one another. The sense of impending loss and danger adds to the fear and risk necessarily involved in such a close friendship between two officers at this time.

In *Regeneration*, Sassoon and Owen also meet as a direct result of the war, but in completely different circumstances to Barton and Hilliard. There is not the same sense of fear involved in their relationship, partly due to the different nature of their friendship. Although Sassoon may, during his conversations with Dr Rivers, express some concerns over the consequences of an officer displaying homosexual tendencies, this did not necessarily apply to his feelings towards Owen. In the course of this novel, the effect of the war, other than to have placed them in Craiglockhart in the first place, is confined more to their future prospects and poetry as throughout most of the novel, we cannot be sure that either man will ever be passed fit to return to the active duty. Studying this relationship through the eyes of the play *Not About Heroes* could lead one to believe that both men felt a great deal more than is expressed in Pat Barker's novel. *Not About Heroes* takes their relationship on further in time, however, so we are able to see its development and the effect of Owen's death on his surviving friend.

In *Journey's End*, the circumstances of the main relationship are different again. Stanhope and Raleigh, had a pre-existing friendship so the entrance of the war into their lives has a profound effect on their relationship. Gone are the days of school cricket and rugby with Stanhope looking after his younger friend. Stanhope, who has been serving for many years, has become war-weary; his personality has changed, almost beyond recognition; his outlook has become tempered by his experiences. Sherriff shows us this disintegration of Stanhope's character through Raleigh's eyes, enabling us to experience his loss of innocence which occurs, in part, as he witnesses his friend's breakdown. Any trust which may have existed between these two before the war is now gone, as Stanhope realises he is no longer the same person that Raleigh used to worship. He cannot live up to Raleigh's high expectations and this only serves to heighten his sense of failure and make him more resentful of Raleigh's presence, as a reminder of the man he once was.

THE EFFECTS OF THE WAR ON THE INDIVIDUAL

The effects of the war on the individual is a popular topic for
comparisons, and is represented in almost every form of literature
within this genre. In *Journey's End*, the most obvious subject is
Stanhope, whose personality has undergone a complete
transformation. The audience only know him as the war-weary,
cynical and embittered man of three year's war experience. Raleigh,
on the other hand, knew him before he underwent these changes
and this is how the audience gets to know of the effects of the war.
The extent of the change in Stanhope's character is so great that
neither man really seems to recognise the other when they first
meet. This is a very simple device, employed by Sherriff, which
enables the audience to understand how complete the
transformation has been. Raleigh's character undergoes a change
too, as he becomes more experienced. He really changes after he
comes back from the raid which has cost Osborne's life. He cannot
understand what has happened to him, and looks to Stanhope for
reassurance, which he does not receive. This shows how, despite
their former friendship, and Stanhope's generally protective nature,
he is no longer able to help his friend - he is simply not capable
anymore.

Sometimes authors portray the consequences of war in the form of
a psychological trauma. This is the case in *The Return of the Soldier*
by Rebecca West. Here, the hero, Chris Baldry has lost his memory
and returned to his family home believing himself still to be twenty-
one years old and in a relationship with his first-love, Margaret. His
wife Kitty is, needless to say, shocked by his behaviour and the story
is concerned with whether Chris should have treatment to bring
him back to reality, or allowed to remain in the, far happier,
world he seems to now inhabit. The reader is not told exactly what
has caused Chris's loss of memory, but it is clear from his changed
appearance that his experiences of the war have taken their toll on

him, both physically and emotionally. This novel not only outlines the effects of the war on the men who served in it, but also the consequences for their families and loved-ones back at home.

Another novel which shows this form of reaction to the war is *Regeneration* by Pat Barker. This story is set in a hospital for officers suffering from war neurosis, and centres mainly on the "curing" of various psychological problems relating to the mens' experiences in the war. Among these is Billy Prior, whose trauma is vividly described during a session of hypnosis. The novel sets out to explore the effects on these men, each of whom seems to have reacted in a different way. Billy Prior has become mute; Burns vomits whenever he is near food and Anderson has developed a morbid fear of the sight of blood, which is even more strange, given that he had been serving as a surgeon. The doctor in charge of these men, Dr W H R Rivers tries to get the men to talk about their experiences, and face their fears in order to lessen their importance. Although not always successful, this brings to light another aspect of the war's consequences as Dr Rivers himself becomes a victim of trauma. His conscience is constantly battling against his perceived duty. He knows that he must try to make the men better, but is also aware that in doing so, they may be sent back to the front and could be killed. Eventually he becomes so worn down by having to deal with the men in is care that he has a breakdown himself.

Not all authors use such obvious methods of demonstrating the effects of war on the individual. In many cases, it is not one single event which has the greatest impact, but a gradual wearing down of the nerves. One good example of this is *All Quiet on the Western Front*, in which Erich Maria Remarque shows how a young man, Paul Bäumer, sees all of his friends and comrades die or be badly wounded until eventually he gives up all hope for his own future. He believes that, if he survives, he may never be able to pick up the threads of his life before the war. This gradual breakdown which takes place during the novel shows how, eventually, everyone - even the most optimistic - reaches a point where they can simply not take any more.

By contrast, the main character in the novel *Birdsong*, Stephen Wraysford, is initially portrayed as comparatively unaffected by his experiences in the war. He is remote and cut-off from the events which are going on around him. This is due to his reaction to the end of his relationship with Isabelle Azaire, which has left him emotionally scarred. His self-imposed isolation ends with the death of his friend, Michael Weir and this episode marks a changing awareness in Stephen as he begins to realise his own capacity to care for his fellow man. Despite the appearance of being emotionally cut-off from his surroundings, the war obviously has an impact on Stephen as the reader later learns that after the war he did not speak for two years. This suggests that he had in fact been deeply affected by the various events he witnessed and he, presumably, felt the need to quietly assimilate and deal with his experiences, before he could begin to communicate again. Sebastian Faulks' intentions in the portrayal of Stephen Wraysford are arguably more complex. Stephen is shown to already have a troubled mind before the war, due to his childhood experiences and his broken relationship with Isabelle. He is portrayed as a man who has made the conscious decision to lock away his emotions and keep them in check, probably for fear of getting hurt again. No-one is allowed to get close to him. This portrayal helps the reader to understand that the effects of the war can be gradual, but are no less devastating than those of a man who experiences a single traumatic event. The person who eventually pulls him back from this emotional void is Jeanne - Isabelle's sister - who helps him to rebuild his life and provides him with much needed stability.

Faulks also shows us how the war could have life-long consequences for those involved. The character of Brennan is seen as a confused and broken man, living in a world of his own in a Star and Garter Home. He has been existing like this for nearly sixty years - in other words since the end of the First World War.

THE EFFECTS OF DEATH AND LOSS ON THE INDIVIDUAL

The ways in which the characters deal with death is as varied as their own personalities and can differ greatly to their general reaction to the war, depending on the circumstances and on their relationship with the person who has died.

In *Journey's End*, Osborne's death is treated differently by the two main characters. Raleigh seems to feel guilty that he has survived while Osborne has died. This is partly because he has come to understand that Osborne was an essential character in Stanhope's life and he feels that he is somehow responsible for his loss. Also, he seems to be deeply affected by what he has witnessed during the raid, he becomes much quieter and more reserved than he had been previously and all of his enthusiasm has gone.

Stanhope, who has lost his best friend, reacts differently. To Raleigh, and the audience it *appears* that Stanhope does not care - he carries on as normal - even having a celebratory meal and joking around with the other officers. This dinner had been planned before the raid - Osborne and Raleigh had discussed it before they went out on their mission. However, during the dinner, there is an air of forced enjoyment as Stanhope tries to avoid discussing the raid or its consequences. To have cancelled the dinner would have been like admitting defeat - a trait not present in Stanhope's character - so the dinner must go ahead and Stanhope uses it as a means to drink and forget. This is because he knows that to think about Osborne's death will stop him functioning. He must continue to perform his duties because his men and the other officers are relying on him. In his nervous state, Stanhope understands that he cannot afford the luxury of grieving for his friend - he would be unable to cope if he actually did dwell on Osborne's death, and would probably fall apart completely.

When Raleigh dies, Stanhope is not given the opportunity to dwell on his schoolfriend's death as he is called upon to meet his own fate, although it is interesting to note that he gently touches Raleigh's head just before leaving the dugout, which seems to be an act of love and tenderness which we have not witnessed in Stanhope before.

Within this theme, one could also look at Raleigh's loss of Stanhope as his hero and friend. Raleigh appears shocked and disturbed by Stanhope's reaction to him and his frequent angry outbursts. Having grown up under Stanhope's protection, Raleigh must now face the destruction of his previously-held opinions. The change in both of these characters on Raleigh's death-bed and the momentary resumption of their old friendship allows Raleigh to die peacefully, with Stanhope heroic nature fully restored in his eyes.

In *Regeneration* Wilfred Owen has to face a different type of loss: he is so bewildered at the prospect of leaving Sassoon that he finds this sense of loss unquantifiable; many of the patients of Craiglockhart are there because they have been unable to cope, mentally, with the losses they have had to experience. Some of them have been permanently wounded, not physically, but psychologically and must learn to come to terms with this. As such, one of the main themes of *Regeneration* is this journey from initial loss to survival - the rebuilding of men.

Strange Meeting is probably one of the hopeful and uplifting pieces of First World War literature, yet the surviving character, Hilliard, has many personal losses to contend with. Not only has his beloved Barton been killed but his own leg has been amputated. Losing Barton has always been Hilliard's worst fear - he has always been unsure, having discovered love and his own capacity for it, that he could carry on living without the object of that love. His dependence on Barton has become paramount and due to this, he feels that the loss of his leg is of secondary importance. His own family hardly know how to react to him, but Barton's family pour out their affection and through this Hilliard is able to face the future. Susan Hill uses Hilliard's reaction to the the loss of Barton to demonstrate that a powerful and deep-rooted love, such as that which exists between these two characters, can overcome any obstacle and is far more long-lasting and ultimately satisfying than a quickly-spent passion.

There is a similar lesson to be learnt in *Birdsong* by Sebastian Faulks. Stephen Wraysford's passionate and illicit affair with Isabelle Azaire ends in his abandonment and forms the basis of his emotionally destroyed character. Throughout the novel, the reader is given the impression that Stephen cares little for his own life, and this remains so until he is faced with the prospect of losing it. During the tunnel scene where Stephen and Jack Firebrace are trapped underground, it is Stephen, rather than the religious Jack, who provides the hope for their future and encourages Jack to live for the sake of his wife. Once Jack is dead and Stephen is faced with his own mortality, he realises that the loss of Isabelle is less important to him than that he should be allowed to continue living. He understands also that Jeanne, Isabelle's sister, provides a hope for his future, and also he must live his life for the sake of all those who have died.

Erich Maria Remarque puts his central character, the young Paul Bäumer in *All Quiet on the Western Front*, through many harrowing experiences of loss. His friends - many of whom he was at school with - all die, until he is the only one left. For Paul, however, the most traumatic of these deaths is not one of his schoolfriends, but his comrade Stanislaus Katczinsky. Paul and Kat (as he is called) are together when Kat is injured. Paul carries his friend to a medical station where the orderly says they are too late - Kat is dead. At this moment Paul feels as if his life has ended: he can no longer feel anything but merely exists from that point onwards. Effectively, his life ceases with the loss of his friend.

Several poets wrote movingly of their grief and facing the future after so many deaths. Edith Nesbit, for example, in *The Fields of Flanders* writes of the debt of gratitude she feels for the sacrifices being demanded of, and made by so many young men. This is a debt which, in her view, can never be repaid. This sentiment is echoed in Wilfrid Wilson Gibson's *Lament* which beautifully evokes his sense of loss. Gibson is asking here how he is supposed to carry on living knowing that so many have given up everything to gain his freedom. This sense of gratitude, mixed with grief and even an element of guilt results in everything he does and sees being tinged with heartbreak - a feeling which he realises he will have to live with for the rest of his life. To Gibson, the pain of such a life is worse than death itself.

Some poets addressed poems to specific people who had died. For example Vera Brittain's poem *Perhaps* is addressed to her fiancé Roland Leighton who died on 23rd December 1915. In this poem she recites, with great sadness, all of the things she will no longer enjoy or will never be able to do, because he is not with her. Siegfried Sassoon's poem *To Any Dead Officer* was originally addressed to Lieutenant E. L. Orme who was killed in action on 27th May 1917. Here, Sassoon reminisces about happier times, when they had laughed together, before going on to describe his friend's death and how pointless it seems. Although, in typical Sassoon style, the poem ends on a note of irony, his emotions are very much on the surface in this piece and his acute sense of loss, which is thinly masked by humour, is profoundly moving. The sense that some were unable to ever forget their war experiences and the losses they suffered, is brought to life in Edmund Blunden's poem *1916 seen from 1921*. Here he describes a tremendous feeling of loss and sadness. The reader becomes acutely aware that he is biding his time, waiting for his life to return to him, so that he can once again be at peace in his beloved countryside, but one also realises that he never really achieved this aim. Like so many others, he was never truly able to forget.

RESPONSIBILITY

Another aspect of the war, which is worthy of examination is that of responsibility - looking after the men. In *Journey's End* it is clear throughout that Stanhope always puts his men first. He regards himself as their father-figure, although in many cases he is much younger than them. He knows and accepts that it is his responsibility to ensure that his men are at their best, both for their own benefit and for the good of the company as a whole.

Pat Barker gives Sassoon's reason for wanting to return to the front in *Regeneration*, as his desire to be back with his men and to be of service to them. He has a strong sense of guilt that he is safe, whilst they are dying in France. Robert Graves points out that this feeling was mutual and, in reality, In reality, Sassoon wrote his poem *Banishment* at this time which portrays his feelings for the men he had left behind, and his desire to right any wrongs he may have done them.

In *Strange Meeting* David Barton, like Stanhope, is quite prepared to discuss his own fears in order to ease those of his men. However, Hilliard's main concern is the welfare of Barton. That is not to say that he doesn't care about the other men in his company, but he knows that, due to his own emotional inadequacies, Barton is better suited and more able to meet their needs. He feels that, for everybody's sake, but especially his own, Barton must be kept safe, and this becomes the main focus of his attention throughout the novel.

These portrayals are quite realistic and the officer commanding a company of men was often expected to be a mother-figure, as well as a father-figure, to his men. It was his responsibility to ensure that the men were fed, washed, had somewhere to sleep, kept their equipment clean etc. In addition, he also had to provide moral support to the men and listen to their problems, trying to help solve them if possible. Given the extreme youth of most of these officers, like Stanhope, it is hardly surprising that they occasionally buckled under the weight of so many demands.

One poet who typified this attitude was E. A. Mackintosh whose love and feelings of responsibility for his men is the main theme of much of his poetry. *In Memoriam* is a particularly good example of this and demonstrates how much like a father-figure he felt, as well as his sense of pride at being the officer in charge of his men, for whom he had a great respect and admiration. The story behind this moving poem is interesting. During a raid, one of Mackintosh's men, Private David Sutherland, was wounded. Mackintosh carried him for some time until it became clear that the young soldier was dead and Mackintosh was forced to leave his body behind in order to help others get back to their trenches. He actually managed to bring in two other men under heavy fire and was awarded the Military Cross for his courage. Despite this, he was overwhelmed by guilt for having left Sutherland's body in No Man's Land and this poem demonstrates his feelings of inadequacy for having, in his own mind, 'failed' this young man.

A QUESTION OF COMPARISONS

Many students have to make direct comparisons between two particular texts, demonstrating the author's treatment of a specific topic. Where this is dealt with as coursework, some examination boards allow that the student may be permitted to choose the texts for themselves. To that end, we have included a list of possible topics and suggested texts which, in our opinion, provide suitable material for such essays, assuming that *Journey's End* will be one of the texts involved.

THE EFFECTS OF THE WAR ON THE INDIVIDUAL

This can take the form of a psychological or emotional response either to the war in general or to a specific event. Students are expected to show an understanding of an author's treatment of this subject.

Using Journey's End and Regeneration

Good examples of this subject matter can be found in Stanhope's character in *Journey's End* and in Billy Prior in *Regeneration* by Pat Barker. Sherriff shows us the disintegration of Stanhope through the eyes of his schoolfriend Raleigh and makes it clear that his problems stem from the length of service he has seen. Billy Prior, on the other hand, has become traumatised by a solitary experience, although during his treatment it becomes clear that his psychological problems are the result of a build-up of distressing happenings.

Stanhope and Prior have different backgrounds and both authors use these backgrounds to demonstrate their characters and show us that their upbringing and education form an integral part of their reactions and behaviour during the war. Students should therefore look at the descriptions of their characters before the war and contrast these with their personalities during the conflict in order to assess the impact of their experiences.

Using Journey's End and Strange Meeting

Raleigh's initial experience of the war during the raid changes him from a young naive adventurer into a shocked and disturbed young man. In Strange Meeting, the character of David Barton undergoes a similar transformation. David Barton is a pleasant, keen and innocent new recruit, who changes following a harrowing spell in the front line trenches.

Susan Hill portrays Barton's reactions in the form of his silence and withdrawal, which contrasts with his previously outgoing character. His close friend Hilliard tries to draw out a response from Barton, and there is a role reversal here, as the formerly quiet, reticent Hilliard helps Barton to adjust to what has happened. Raleigh, on the other hand, is clearly keen to discuss his experiences with Stanhope, who is incapable of assisting him.

In this instance, there are several characters and reactions to examine: Stanhope and Hilliard, who have not directly experienced these traumatic events themselves react differently to their friends' requirements. Barton and Raleigh are both traumatised by what they have seen, but they respond differently. Students should look at the relationships portrayed between the individuals and assess their influence on the outcome.

THE PRESENTATION OF HEROISM

Students can take several different views of this subject, from hero-worship, to a man's perception of heroism or courage - whether his own, or that of someone else.

Using Journey's End and Regeneration

When looking at hero worship, an excellent example can be found in the feelings of Raleigh for Stanhope. This emotion forms the basis of their relationship and students should also pay attention to Stanhope's reaction to Raleigh's arrival. Stanhope, it would seem, had taken his heroic status quite seriously while at school and feels under extreme pressure to continue with this at the front.

In *Regeneration*, Pat Barker has used the real-life relationship between Siegfried Sassoon and Wilfred Owen to show how strong the feeling of hero-worship can be. Owen is in awe of his older friend and, when the two part, his loss is almost incalculable.

Using these two books to demonstrate heroism, or the perception of heroism, is equally viable. In *Journey's End*, many of the characters are given heroic traits. Osborne, for example, faces the raid with an outward calm which is quite remarkable. He is an experienced officer who has undertaken such tasks in the past, and yet he approaches this mission with an inspiring level-headedness. Stanhope's understanding of courage and heroism is also worth noting here. He feels he has failed, and in turning to alcohol for courage, he feels disappointed that his nerves have let him down. However, throughout the play, we are shown that this is not the case. Although his three years of traumatic service have taken their toll, he never lacks courage and always puts the wellbeing and safety of others before himself.

Most of the characters in *Regeneration*, are in Craiglockhart hospital because of either a mental or physical breakdown and many of them display true courage in facing up to their fears and trying to return to a normal life. Billy Prior's perception of his own trauma is to not believe that something so 'insignificant' could have caused him to breakdown. Like Stanhope, he believes that his nerves have failed him and appears disappointed in his own courage. Rivers must help him to rebuild his self-confidence and face the future.

Using Journey's End and Birdsong

When comparing these two pieces, the nature of the heroism involved is more that of rising above one's circumstances. For example, the character of Trotter in *Journey's End* seems to not show any fear or feelings at all for the situation in which he has found himself. This demonstrates a true courage: to appear to carry on almost as normal despite his circumstances, which shows us the true nature of Trotter's character - the down to earth soldier, who simply gets on with the job at hand. Sherriff's use of Trotter to this end, forces the audience to realise that heroism is not all about dashing around 'appearing' brave, but has much more to do with facing fear every day, and carrying on regardless.

In *Birdsong*, the central character, Stephen Wraysford also seems to keep going, regardless. In this instance, however, Sebastian Faulks is using this to demonstrate Wraysford's numbness - he simply does not feel anything due to his emotional torment following Isabelle's abandonment of him. Isabelle herself shows an element of bravery when she falls in love with a German soldier, knowing that this will necessitate her rejection by everyone she holds dear. She knowingly abandons her life in France to be with Max, realising that she will never be able to return again.

In addition, Sebastian Faulks shows us a character who manages to overcome a terrible personal loss and yet continue with his duties.

Jack Firebrace, the tunneller, loses his son, but still manages to keep going and perform the tasks he is set. Eventually Jack does succumb to death, but only after he has faced the very worst that life has to throw at him, and to rise above it.

Students who approach this topic should bear in mind that 'heroism' or 'courage' had very different meanings before and during the First World War to a modern-day perception, when we are apt to give famous footballers or screen idols a heroic status. The characters in these pieces must face their own fears or their own potential deaths, in the full knowledge of the consequences.

THE EFFECTS OF THE WAR ON MALE RELATIONSHIPS

Within this topic, students can choose whether to focus on relationships which pre-existed the war, or those which have been formed during, and because of, the conflict.

Using Journey's End and All Quiet on the Western Front
In both of these cases, the authors use both types of male relationship mentioned above. In *Journey's End*, Raleigh and Stanhope had known each other before the war, but Stanhope's greatest friendship is with Osborne, a man much older and wiser than himself, upon whom he has come to depend. Stanhope's friendship with Raleigh is, of necessity, completely different to the one they shared at school, which Raleigh finds difficult to accept.

A similar situation occurs in *All Quiet on the Western Front*. Here Paul Bäumer is serving at the front with many of his schoolfriends, but his greatest ally is a man twice his age, whom he only met once he had enlisted: Stanislaus Katczinsky. One by one, Paul's friends are killed, or seriously injured, but it is Kat's death which has the greatest impact on him. He literally cannot see the point in going on any longer.

Stanhope's reaction to Osborne's death is different: although he is naturally deeply affected, he cannot simply stop. As an officer, too many other people are relying on him for him to allow himself the luxury of grieving. Herein lies one of he fundamental contrasts between these two books and how the authors deal with emotional elements. The characters in *Journey's End* are all officers, mainly from the upper classes, and therefore to openly show emotions would not have been acceptable behaviour. In *All Quiet on the Western Front*, however, the central characters are all ranking soldiers, whose emotions are allowed to the surface. Remarque's story is told through the eyes of Paul Bäumer, who forms an attachment to a 'father-figure'. Sherriff, on the other hand, whilst acknowledging Stanhope's need for Osborne, never allows the audience to forget who is the most senior officer.

Using Journey's End and Strange Meeting

These two works contain different types of relationship, and both of them show how the war can impact greatly. In *Journey's End*, the relationship between Raleigh and Stanhope is adversely affected by Raleigh's arrival in Stanhope's Company. Until that point, Raleigh had only been a memory of schooldays for Stanhope, as well as being the brother of Madge and both of these were things he had chosen not to think about too much. Raleigh's arrival serves to remind Stanhope of everything that he has lost. The war's impact on this relationship is to almost fracture it completely. Stanhope cannot accept Raleigh's presence until the very end when Raleigh is dying. It is only at this point that Stanhope can lower his guard and allow his former personality to come through to the aid of his young friend.

Conversely, in *Strange Meeting*, the relationship between Barton and Hilliard only starts as a direct result of the war. These two characters had no previous knowledge of one another and come from very different family backgrounds. The fact that they fall in love during the war shows that not all of the effects of the conflict are negative. In fact, Susan Hill's portrayal of this relationship is probably one of the more hopeful and deeply affecting pieces of First World War literature. The reader is left with the overriding impression that love can conquer absolutely everything - even death.

One of the main reasons behind the differences in these two pieces could be the time at which they were written. *Journey's End* was first performed in 1928 while *Strange Meeting* was published in 1971. As stated earlier in this guide, this time difference allowed Susan Hill a far greater freedom to hint at a homosexual relationship between her main characters than would have been afforded to R C Sherriff. However, Susan Hill does not choose to openly mention homosexuality. She leaves this to the reader's imagination and prefers instead to portray a close, loving and intense relationship which has been brought about because of the war, rather than being ruined by it.

THE ACCRINGTON PALS
BY PETER WHELAN

INTRODUCTION

First performed in 1981, this play tells of the formation, service and eventual decimation of the Accrington Pals, one of many such battalions founded as a result of Kitchener's call to arms in 1914.

Interwoven with this story of a town's loss, is the personal story of two of its characters. One is an individualist, a young woman seeking to make her own way in the world, not to rely on others, but to take responsibility for her own future. The other is an idealist, a believer in the collective good. He thinks that everyone has a duty to take care of their fellow man.

This unlikely couple form a friendship, which slowly and falteringly blossoms into romance. It is their misfortune to have met at a time when personal beliefs and feelings had to take second place to the nation's needs - which cost the lives of so many.

Saturday 26th September 1914: The Battalion, led by Col R Sharples and the
'Accrington Old Band', parades through Accrington town centre before the Mayor
and raiser of the Battalion, John Harwood JP.
(Image Ref: WT400)
Image courtesy of William Turner Collection, Lancashire County Library and Information Service

SYNOPSIS

ACT ONE

Scene One

It is Autumn 1914 and Tom Hackford enters, pulling a green-grocer's cart and begins to get it ready for the early-morning customers. He is joined by May Hassal, who seems surprised that Tom has managed to get out of bed at all. After a while, May mentions Tom's behaviour the previous night, to which she has clearly taken some offence. It would seem that Tom had returned home very late and quite drunk. May believes that she heard Tom call out that he would be glad to go away, to be free of her. Tom tries to assure May that she misheard him: he had really said that he would be glad to be away from the town. May's anger eventually subsides, although it is clear that she disapproves of him enlisting, believing it to be a waste of his life.

They are interrupted by the arrival of Arthur Boggis. He is going around the streets, waking up the mill-workers [a knocker-up was often employed by the factories to ensure that their workers woke up and got to work on time]. This is not normally Arthur's job, but he is covering for another man who is unwell. He stops for a short chat before passing on. Then his son, Reggie arrives, announcing that he has been out all night and is trying to avoid his mother, who will be angry with him. Reggie leaves again and Tom's friend Ralph enters. He seems to think that Tom will have asked a favour of May, but it would appear that Tom has not yet had the opportunity. Eva Mason arrives and an embarrassing scene ensues: Tom should have asked May if Eva could take over his job on the stall, and his room in May's house. May is, however, unaware of this and both she and Eva feel awkward, but May quickly agrees that Eva can stay, although she is angry with Tom for not mentioning the situation beforehand.

Reggie's mother, Annie Boggis appears in search of her son, followed by one of the mill-workers, Sarah Harding. Reggie approaches his mother, who is extremely angry with him. Another mill-worker, Bertha Treecott, enters and, while she and Sarah wait for their fruit, they comment on the domestic argument unfolding before them. Eva is quite shocked by Annie's violence, but the others explain that this is quite normal behaviour. Everyone is relieved when the factory hooters sound to mark the beginning of the working day.

Later, Eva and May are alone, clearing away the stall and discussing the men who have enlisted. Eva is supportive of their decision, but May believes that the unemployed should have gone first. Eva is keen to stay with May and help on the stall, although, as May points out, times are hard and she can barely make ends meet. They briefly talk about Eva's relationship with Ralph, which May seems to believe might be closer than Eva admits. May gives Eva a less than favourable account of life in the town and it becomes apparent that May is ambitious to better herself. Eva reminds May that she will miss Tom and that she had gone to the recruiting office to plead for him not to have to go to the war.

Scene Two

This scene depicts May's memories of her visit to the recruiting office where she met Company Sergeant Major Rivers, to whom she had appealed for Tom's release from military service. She had tried very hard to make Rivers see things from her perspective - explaining how young and impressionable Tom is and that he was goaded into joining up: she had even offered to pay Rivers for Tom's release. The CSM had been unyielding: Tom had signed on and was keen to do his bit. He had politely suggested to May that she should concentrate on running her business and leave Tom's welfare to the army. May had eventually been forced to accept that there was nothing more she could do and had left, disappointed.

Scene Three

Back in the present, Bertha, Sarah and Eva are standing by the stall discussing the way the local men have changed since they joined-up. Bertha says that she wishes she could do more to help with the war effort, although Sarah believes the war will be over before the men have even completed their training. They are joined by Ralph and Bertha relates a story she has read in the newspaper about German atrocities in Belgium. Tom arrives and Ralph reminds him that he had promised to draw a sketch of Eva, so Tom promptly begins a drawing. The Boy's Brigade band can be heard in the background, ready to see the troops off. Reggie and his parents enter, and as ever, Annie is scolding her son because he should be playing with the band, but is running late. Arthur is in uniform, ready to depart with all the other men and is carrying one of his prized homing pigeons, named England's Glory. He is planning to take the bird with him to France. He suggests that they should all join together and say a prayer.

The time has come for the men to go to the station, but May, who had arrived quietly a few minutes earlier, refuses to go and see them off. Everyone departs, leaving Tom and May alone. He suggests that he could find an excuse not to go, but May is still too angry with him to really acknowledge this. She offers him some money, which he refuses. An awkward silence follows before Tom tries to embrace May. She rejects him forcefully and he leaves, angry at her cold attitude.

Scene Four

Time has moved on and it is now winter. Eva and Sarah sit in May's kitchen while Eva reads a poem from the local newspaper. Sarah is concerned that May will be angry to find her sitting in the kitchen, but then remembers that May will be late because she will have gone to Peel Park to sell goods to the upper-class ladies who live there. Eva admits that she misses Ralph and the two women are happily enjoying their chat when May returns. Much to Sarah's surprise, May is not angry, but seems to be in a much better mood than the other two had expected. While she makes the tea, May reveals that she has received a letter from Tom, which appears to be the cause of her cheery mood. Sarah leaves and May and Eva discuss Eva's day at work. Then May divulges that she has been looking at premises, with a view to expanding her business. She recalls her upbringing and her family's fall from prosperity. While they are both in a confiding mood, Eva lets slip that she and Ralph have slept together. May is surprised, but not unduly shocked and they then move on to the topic of her and Tom. May denies that she has any feelings for Tom and quickly changes the subject again. She tells Eva that one of her upper-class customers, a Mrs Dickenson, has shown an interest in hearing Eva sing at one of her charity concerts. May seems keen that Eva should perform as it will advance her own reputation. They both look forward to the men coming home on leave, although May anticipates that Tom will go to his aunt in Salford.

Scene Five

Tom is on guard duty at the training camp. He is joined by CSM Rivers who gives him some advice about being on guard. They then discuss May for a short while until Rivers turns the conversation around to comradeship and loyalty, reminding Tom that others are relying on him to do his duty and not let them down.

Scene Six

Tom and Ralph are on leave. Ralph and Eva are upstairs while Tom and May sit in the kitchen, trying to hide their embarrassment at the obvious antics which are taking place in Eva's bedroom. May seems surprised that Tom has chosen to spend his leave with her, rather than his aunt. He does not really answer this, but instead begins to praise the army for its ability to allow the men to function without money. He sees it as a fair exchange that a man should get his board and lodging in return for the use of any skills he might have. May perceives this ideology as naive. As they move closer, however, May becomes nervous and when Tom tries to take her hand, she once again rejects him. Just before she leaves the room, she asks Tom to draw a picture of her before he goes back to the camp. They embrace and May wishes that they were meeting now for the first time, with Tom as a man, rather than the innocent boy she recalls from his first arrival.

Scene Seven

Arthur has written a letter home to Jack, the man he had replaced on knocking-up duty. Arthur reveals that the battalion has moved to Ripon. This letter shows Arthur as a very religious man, who seems to feel that the war is God's way of cleansing the earth of its sins.

Scene Eight

Time has moved on and it is the winter of 1915. Sarah, Bertha and Eva, at the stall, discuss Bertha' new job as a tram conductress. Bertha says that the men that she works with do not treat her very well. Eva thinks this is because the men are frightened of women taking over their jobs. A minor disagreement follows as Eva tries to defend the men, while Sarah takes the side of the working women. This is broken up by the entrance of Annie Boggis, who is, once again, searching for Reggie. Sarah and Annie argue over Annie's behaviour towards her son and she gleefully tells them that she has discovered that the men are being sent to France. May, who had discreetly entered during the argument, confirms that this is true. Sarah and Bertha go, followed by Annie. Eva is worried about Ralph and May tries to reassure her, while blaming herself for having been so harsh to Tom.

Scene Nine

It is a few weeks later and Tom and Ralph are once again on leave. Ralph is taking a bath in the kitchen, while Tom mends a pair of May's shoes. Eva joins them and helps Ralph, although her presence obviously makes Tom feel uncomfortable. When May returns, there is an awkward scene, although Tom reassures her that nothing improper had happened as he had been present. May, in an effort to be more friendly to Tom, praises his work on her shoes and he goes off to borrow some wax from a neighbour. May tells Eva that she has brought a rabbit home for their dinner. Ralph offers to skin the rabbit in return for being allowed to share it with them. May agrees and while Ralph is doing this, she tells Eva that she is confused about her feelings for Tom. Eva assures her that Tom is in love with her. Although May is still unsure, she is clearly flattered and begins to wonder how matters will progress, when Tom enters with

Reggie, who is bleeding. They all attend to him and when he is more calm it becomes clear that he has had a fit. They also learn that his mother had hit him with the buckle end of a belt.

May seems less willing than the others to help Reggie: she is worried about how Annie might react to any interference. May speaks to Reggie and tells him to say to his mother that he is now working for May on the stall. Reggie leaves and is quickly followed by Tom, who is unhappy at May's actions. There is an angry exchange between them before Tom departs. Although she is initially reticent, May goes after him to persuade him to come back.

Scene Ten

Outside, May looks around for Tom, only to come face-to-face with CSM Rivers. He tells May that Tom has already left for the station. He speaks of the pride which the men have in their home town and in each other. May is angry and leaves.

Main Points of Interest in Act One

THE CHARACTERS

• All of the main characters are introduced early in Act One. The audience learns about their backgrounds and opinions on various matters.

• May's and Tom's characters are fleshed out, and their faltering relationship begins to show signs of blossoming, although their different attitudes always seem to come between them.

THE PALS

• The men display different perspectives and reactions to having enlisted, and towards the war in general. Once they have departed for France, however, they seem more bored than anything, although they have not really seen any action yet.

• The women also have different points of view about their menfolk joining up. These range from Eva's fear for Ralph's safety, to May's anger at the waste of valuable young lives.

WORKING WOMEN

• All of the women featured in the play are working. Some of them, as the story progresses, take on positions vacated by the men who have gone to fight.

• The women show different reactions to their new role in society and the changes which taking place in their lives.

ACT TWO

Scene One

This scene opens with Ralph, now in France, reading a letter which he has written to Eva. It is just before the beginning of the Battle of the Somme and Ralph has written this letter as a confession to Eva, although he does not believe she will ever receive it. In this letter, as well as describing how he feels about the anticipated attack, he also admits to having slept with some prostitutes while he has been away. He feels guilty about this and wishes he could be at home with Eva.

Back in May's kitchen, Eva is sewing her outfit for the charity concert. May comes in, tired and hot from doing her deliveries in Peel Park. Eva had been planning to go to the pub with Sarah and Bertha, but May announces that she has invited the others round to her house. Both women are in the mood for a celebration as they believe that the battle which is about to start in France will bring about the end of the war. May is feeling extra cheerful because she thinks she has found a shop which she could take over. Much to Eva's surprise, May suggests that they become partners in the new business venture. Eva is concerned, however, that May only wants her to be involved because she will eventually marry Ralph and then Tom will also come back. May is hurt by this accusation which she feels is unfair.

Scene Two

Tom reads a letter which he has written to May. He thanks her for the food parcel she had sent to him and tells her about the comradeship between the men. He has done some sketches of his friends and has enclosed these with his letter. He tells her that he is trying to draw a picture of her from some photographs which he has.

Scene Three

The four women are enjoying their get-together in May's kitchen. They are singing, dancing and drinking beer. Sarah announces that Bertha has a boyfriend who is an asthmatic electrician. Because of his illness he has failed his medical examination and been unable to enlist. Bertha says that, despite his attentions, she could never love a man who had not gone to fight. Eva, Bertha and Sarah talk about their men, but May's attitude becomes harsh: she disapproves of the way women conduct themselves. She suddenly realises how drunk she is and excuses herself. As Sarah and Bertha prepare to leave, they discuss with Eva how strained her relationship with May has become lately.

Scene Four

The scene changes to the trenches, just before the attack. Ralph and Tom are together and, while Ralph adjusts his pack and talks about the forthcoming attack, Tom ponders about workers' rights and who should lead them. As they are ordered to get ready, Ralph becomes nervous. Arthur, who is also with them, talks to his pigeon. CSM Rivers joins the men, with last-minute advice - paying special attention to Tom. Arthur seems to have lost his faith in God, as his prayer no longer praises God, but blames Him for what has happened. As they go over-the-top, the scene changes and the audience sees Eva singing at the charity concert. She forgets the words of her song and runs off the stage - angry with herself.

Scene Five

Sarah is in her back yard, hanging out washing when Annie appears, looking for Reggie, who eventually arrives. Annie is cross with her son for telling rude rhymes to some of the local children. Bertha runs in carrying the local newspaper and shouting that the war is over. May and Eva join them and Sarah reads from the newspaper. The women are all delighted and relieved: they start celebrating. May takes the newspaper and reads an article about the charity concert. It would seem that Eva's mistake has been interpreted as her becoming over-emotional during the singing of such a patriotic song. May is pleased by this and while they discuss it, Annie notices a pigeon approaching, which she believes to be England's Glory - the bird which Arthur had taken to France. Initially, the others try to convince her that the bird could not have found its way back from France, but she remains certain. Eva agrees to fetch the pigeon so they can check whether it is carrying a message, but they find nothing and Eva takes it away. Annie becomes hysterical in her belief that this must mean that Arthur is dead. Reggie arrives and takes his mother home, as she is becoming more and more distraught.

Scene Six

In May's kitchen, Eva acts out Ralph's bath again - she obviously believes that he too is dead. May enters and chastises her friend for this behaviour. She shows Eva a newspaper report where there is no mention of the Accrington Pals having suffered great casualties and hopes that this will quell Eva's fears. The two women argue and Eva goes to strike May, who angrily tells her to leave.

Scene Seven

Reggie is helping May on the stall. She enquires about his mother, who it would seem has suffered a complete breakdown. May tells him to go home and look after Annie. Bertha arrives, looking for

Sarah. The two women have been trying to glean more information about the casualties. Sarah suddenly appears and tells the others, including Eva, who has just arrived, that there are only seven of the Pals left alive. They agree that they should all march to the town hall the next morning to discover the truth from the Mayor. May disagrees and Eva leaves her.

Once alone, May begins to believe that she can see Tom. She says that she is not afraid but she wants to know whether or not he is dead. CSM Rivers appears to her and says that he is looking after Tom and that over 100 men survived - not seven as the women believed. May asks to use his rifle and he shows her how. As she takes aim, Tom appears in the shadows before her and she shoots him. He does not fall, however, because he is already dead. Rivers tells May how Tom died: heroically defending his friends. May is distraught that Tom has thrown away his promising life. Rivers tells Tom that it is time for them to go. May is now so sorry and reaches out to Tom who touches her hands before passing on his way.

Scene Eight

May and Reggie are at the stall, although May seems to be in a dream-like state - not really aware of what is happening around her. Eva enters, carrying her suitcase. She is leaving to go to her sister, who needs help. May is sad to see her friend go, but refuses to accompany her to the bus stop. She asks Eva to read a poem from the newspaper, which she does with some reluctance. Eva then leaves May and Reggie, who return to their work on the stall.

Main Points of Interest in Act Two

DEVELOPING RELATIONSHIPS

- The relationship between Eva and May begins to show signs of disintegrating. Their differences are becoming more obvious - especially with regard to the fate of the men in France.
- May is secretly worried about Tom and after the news from France begins to look very bad, he appears to her, in spirit form. She blames herself for what has happened to him.

REACTIONS TO THE NEWS

- When the news appears to be good, the women celebrate. However, as the truth comes to light, Annie - who had always seemed a harsh woman - reacts badly. She suffers a breakdown once she believes that her husband will not be returning.
- Many of the women join together to march to the town hall and discover the truth about the men. This is the sort of collectivism of which Tom would have approved. May, however, declines to take part - she will find out on her own.
- Once they have discovered the truth, the main female characters react differently: Eva is angry, while May seems to be in a trance - initially unable to function in her normal way. The poem which May wants to hear speaks of pride at the deaths of the town's men - which is not how May had felt before.

June 1915: Pals marching through Accrington Centre past the Town Hall
and the Mayor, in full regalia.
(Image Ref: WT3)
Image courtesy of William Turner Collection, Lancashire County Library and Information Service

CHARACTERS

MAY HASSAL

May appears to be a harsh, strong woman, in her late twenties or early thirties. Her background is very different from the life she now leads and one of her main priorities is to better herself; to regain some of the status which her family had previously held. She knows that most of the other characters do not really like her, but she is not too worried by this, as she has no intention of standing still - she wants to move on in the world. She has little patience for those who lack ambition, or for others who dream their lives away, rather than getting on with things.

May's upbringing has a great impact on her attitude. Her family had been fairly well-to-do, until her father had lost his job and set in motion their downfall. It is clear that May views herself as a cut above the girls who work in the mill and it is this sense of superiority which fuels her ambition to escape her current surroundings.

One of May's strongest characteristics is her fierce sense of independence. She believes that women should be treated in the same way as men, especially as they are taking on so much of the men's work. May has set high standards for herself, but she also seems to expect others to behave with the same decorum as she exhibits. Every so often, however, she lets her guard down and it becomes clear that many of her actions and opinions are actually a cover for the real May, who seems to be quite lonely. Despite her bravado, she appears pleased to have Eva's company and is genuinely sorry when Eva has to leave.

May's relationship with Tom is far more complex. He is ten years younger than May and, although this does not seem to bother him, she feels that this age-gap is a major stumbling block in their relationship. Although, on the surface, May seems not to care about Tom, especially at the beginning of the play, this is clearly not the case. She had gone to the recruiting office to try to persuade the authorities to refuse Tom's enlistment and she seems to resent the fact that he is leaving her. When he comes home on leave for the first time, she warms to him, but ultimately he is once again rejected. Her admission here is interesting as it would appear that she is held back by her memories of how immature Tom had been when he first arrived. She wishes that they were meeting now for the first time.

During Tom's next leave, however, May decides that she will take the initiative and decides to suggest that he should sleep with her. Nevertheless, circumstances prevent this from happening and they part angrily.

May's attachment to Tom is made more complicated by her feelings of guilt. She feels responsible for him while he is alive and, having pushed him away, she feels as though she is to blame for his death. This is demonstrated most particularly in Act 2, Scene 7 which is a dream-like re-enactment of Tom's death, during which it is May who shoots him. May seems to have conflicting emotions about Tom; rejecting him one minute, then reacting angrily when she feels he is being critical of her, and this confusion may be a reflection of the times through which they are living. For the women in the play, their lives are undergoing great upheavals as they come to terms with the changes brought about by the war. With the exception of the ladies who live at Peel Park, most of the women work and their roles in society and the workplace are changing. May's independence and ambition cause others to wonder about her motives and although she clearly loves Tom, it is equally clear that she will allow nothing to stand in the way of her own progress. This might seem like a harsh attitude, but many women began to question traditional values and re-evaluate their position in society during the First World War.

Despite the fact that May has ambitious plans for the future, her feet are firmly on the ground. She is realistic about her relationship with Tom, anticipating that their age-gap might cause problems. She also understands the social strata and realises that, only by her own hard work, will she be able to better herself. She keeps her head when all the others believe the rumours about the number of dead and, while they march to the town hall demanding answers, she remains behind. Once she is alone, however, she gives in to her own fears which demonstrates that, at least some of her actions take the form of a performance for the benefit of the others. In reality, she is desperately worried about Tom, but she refuses to let the other women see a chink in her armour, believing that this would be a sign of weakness. In addition, May refuses to act collectively - she prefers to find things out for herself, rather than join with others. This shows her independence, but also reflects her rejection of Tom's stance on the power of acting as a group with a shared goal, rather than as individuals.

May's attitude to the charity concert is also interesting. She is keen for Eva to participate, despite her new friend's reluctance, because she believes it will enhance her own reputation within the community. Her willingness to fawn to the ladies at Peel Park shows another of the complexities of May's character. She believes in her own independence and superiority, but knows that she must nurture the upper-class ladies if she wants her business to prosper. This sort of contradictory character trait comes across in May's personality throughout the play, as she hides her emotions from everyone, sometimes even herself. This is demonstrated particularly well in her relationship with Tom, which lacks the intimacy shared by Eva and Ralph. On the one hand May obviously has a lot of self respect and refuses to 'give' herself to a man, yet believes that, due to their age gap, she would be ruining *Tom's* life, rather than her own, if they were to be together.

May is a very private person, who keeps herself to herself and expects others to do likewise. She does not interfere in other people's lives and does not appreciate it if they pry too much into her affairs. Her aloof attitude makes her unpopular amongst the other working girls and eventually drives a wedge between her and Eva.

Tom's death has a great impact on May. She becomes more introspective, examining her own role in Tom's life and death. She feels guilty for allowing him to go to the war and for rejecting his affections, but she is also angry that he went to fight in the first place. Following his death, May seems to fall into a dream-like state, hardly aware of what is happening around her. She appears to have lost her ambition and her high opinions of herself, along with her hopes for the future, settling back into her old life and making do.

TOM HACKFORD

At the beginning of the play, Tom is a 19-year-old apprentice who lodges at May's house and has done since before her father died. He helps May with the fruit and vegetable stall, although he has recently joined up and, like the other new recruits, is about to start his training. May refers to him as a dreamer, which is how he seems to her, but this reflects her attitude, rather than his. May believes that people have to help themselves, while Tom has more faith in collective good: that people, acting as a group, are stronger and can ensure a better standard of living for everyone. His ideas are, however, somewhat impractical, given his situation, and this fuels May's argument that he is being unrealistic.

Tom does not see himself as a leader, but goes along with the others. He enlists with his friends, gets drunk with his friends and eventually dies with them too. Despite this, his beliefs are so strong that one can imagine him turning to a life in politics or social reform, if he had survived the war. To him, his ideas are not dreams, but a realistic hope for a better, more equal, future for everyone.

Although May continually decries Tom's 'dreamy' opinions, he proves that he actually has quite a strong, mature and reliable character. He shows that he is good in an emergency when Reggie has a fit, by bringing him to May and trying to help, despite May's protests to the contrary. He feels uncomfortable at Ralph and Eva's open affection - finding it embarrassing to be present while they are carrying on. Finally, in the trench, before the men go over the top, he remains calm and Ralph looks to him for moral support.

Despite his youth, Tom is a proud man. He refuses to accept May's help or money. He seems to resent her offers of assistance, perhaps feeling that she is treating him like a child, when he really wants her to treat him like a man. In other ways, however, he is quite an innocent. His movements towards May, for example, are invariably awkward. This slight clumsiness might not be merely indicative of his youth: it might also demonstrate the strength of his feelings for May. He clearly loves her very much and wants to be with her, but is always unsure of her reactions. This insecurity, coupled with his obvious need for her, makes him behave even more awkwardly. He is in a difficult position in his relationship with May. Ordinarily, as the man, he would expect to take the lead. However, May's age and the fact that she is his landlady make him defer to her. His conduct is always 'gentlemanly', but his confusion over her reactions is obvious and this is hardly surprising, given how confused she is herself.

He thinks nothing of the age-gap between himself and May - in fact it never seems to enter his head that this might cause a problem for them. His occasional bitter outbursts towards May stem from her dismissal of his advances, or their disagreements over politics and society. Despite their differences and her rejection of him, he remains loyal and eager to please her. When he is on leave, rather than going to visit his aunt or going out with his friends, he mends her boots and is keen to impress her by doing the best job he possibly can.

Despite his belief that he is unsuited to the role of leader, Tom eventually proves that this is a task which he could easily have undertaken. When the men are in the trenches, he is the one with a clear head, showing a great deal of maturity in the face of almost certain death. In the final dream-like scene between May and CSM Rivers, it would seem that, in the final moments of his life, Tom had been overwhelmed by the injustice of his friends dying. He had struck out heroically against the enemy and, in doing so, had given his own life.

CSM RIVERS

Company Sergeant Major Rivers is a curious, yet vital character in the play. Appearing initially in May's imagination, as she remembers her visit to the recruiting office, he frequently crops up just at a point where either May or Tom are beginning to question their role within the war. At their first meeting, Rivers appears to May as the voice of officialdom, pointing out that Tom cannot retract his enlistment without a sound reason. He presents May with all sorts of reasons why she should allow Tom to do what he wants. He promises to take special care of Tom, which helps to assuage May's fears.

Rivers seems to know a great deal about May and Tom, although neither had met Rivers before. This gives his character a unearthly air, as though he is not quite real. He is self-assured and confident, but also kindly and considerate. Whenever he is present, he controls the scene and nothing that May says or does has any influence on him. This enhances his ethereal quality - it is like he is not really there, but merely part of May's or Tom's subconsciousness.

At the front line, he looks after Tom, giving him advice and encouragement. Although he asks after May, he is keen to remind Tom of his duty to his fellow soldiers and how much they are relying on him. Once Tom walks out of May's house, he appears, again almost from nowhere, to reassure May that Tom is doing the right thing. Whilst May is unconvinced by Rivers's arguments, nothing that she has to say changes his viewpoint. One could argue that Rivers represents May's conscience: deep down she knows that Tom must do his duty, despite her reluctance to accept this. He also seems to represent Tom's sense of duty, reminding him of his responsibilities and encouraging him before the battle.

Rivers's final appearance comes, once again, in May's imagination. He and Tom are both dead and he tries to reassure May that Tom died a hero, attempting to get to her accept Tom's death and the manner of it. Despite the presence of Tom's ghost, Rivers controls the situation, refusing to listen to May's protests that Tom has thrown away his life, or to condemn her for her perceived part in his death.

The proposition that Rivers is not a 'real' character is reinforced by the fact that Tom and May never talk about him. Whilst this does not give conclusive evidence as to the reality of his character, it is an indication that the role of Rivers could be interpreted as a subliminal one, helping the two main characters accept their situations and also assisting the audience in their understanding of the times.

MINOR CHARACTERS

As with most works of literature, the minor characters, while not necessarily vital to the plot, are there for a reason. In the case of *The Accrington Pals*, these less-involved personalities are used to demonstrate the various attitudes of people at that time. So, for example, Sarah and Bertha represent working-class women, whose lives are undergoing substantial changes due to the war. Sarah's marriage has never been happy, but she had previously accepted her lot in life. Now, as her role in society is having to change, she becomes more outspoken about her marriage and her husband. Bertha, on the other hand, has a different outlook. She is happy to take on the role of the men who have gone to war, but she still holds firm to her belief that it is a man's responsibility to fight and protect his homeland. She states that she could never love a man who had not done his duty.

Eva, as the newcomer, has most to learn about her new environment and her role changes throughout the play. Her involvement with Ralph shows how women's attitudes to sexual relations were changing. May's character represents a more repressed, conventional age, when women waited for marriage, while Eva believes in living for today, rather than waiting for something that might never happen. Her role within the workplace is representative of the inequality of the times. She carries out a man's work, but is not paid the same as a man would be and she also knows that when the men return, she will be expected to give up her job. Both she and May can see the injustice of this, but neither of them would really be prepared to act upon it.

The Boggis family seem fairly dysfunctional. Arthur appears to be a loner, enjoying the company of his pigeons and clinging to his faith. Annie is a hard woman, continually beating and reprimanding her son. She does not take kindly to criticism from the other women.

Reggie is, initially, seen as a mischievous boy, whose sole purpose in life seems to be to annoy his mother. Their lives probably undergo the greatest changes as a result of their involvement in the war. Arthur completely gives up his faith in God, finding it hard to believe that the carnage which he is witnessing in France can be the work of a loving God. Annie suffers a complete breakdown when she hears of her husband's death, showing that she may have been more attached to him than anyone had previously thought. Reggie, who has never really had to be responsible for anything in the past, is forced to take over and become the head of the household.

THE HISTORY OF THE ACCRINGTON PALS

When the First World War began on 4th August 1914, there was a general air in Great Britain, as in much of Europe, of patriotism and excitement. Almost immediately, Lord Kitchener was appointed as Secretary of State for War and his experiences in the Sudan and the Boer War made him believe that the forthcoming conflict was likely to be a long and costly one. He believed that a very large number of men would be required to defeat the German army and, as conscription was not politically acceptable at that time, he began a recruitment campaign to encourage the nation's men to volunteer. The government opened recruiting offices and army camps sprang up all over the country to train the new recruits.

Although the initial response was enthusiastic, the government and army continued to look for new ways to persuade young men to enlist. General Sir Henry Rawlinson, a senior army commander, suggested that men might be more inclined to join up if it could be guaranteed that they would know the men with whom they would be serving.

On 28th August, Lord Derby gave a stirring speech in Liverpool, urging local men to enlist together, to form a 'Battalion of Pals'. His call was answered and within ten days over 3,000 men had joined up, giving Liverpool not one, but three Pals Battalions. This achievement was widely reported in the press and, in towns and cities all over the country, local authorities applied to Lord Kitchener for permission to form their own Battalions of Pals. Some were made up of men who worked together, while others were formed from men who belonged to the same clubs or sports groups. In either case, however, especially in the battalions which were formed in the smaller towns, the men all lived in close proximity and were familiar with each other and their families.

In the Lancashire town of Accrington, there was a secondary incentive to enlist: the town was experiencing extreme hardship due to a decline in the cotton industry, upon which it traditionally relied. Men had been laid off and many families were suffering in conditions of severe poverty. The nationalistic fervour and desire to serve their country was fuelled by the financial benefit of a regular income from the army.

By 24th September a full-strength battalion had been formed from men in Accrington and the surrounding towns and villages. They began their training in nearby camps, before leaving for Caernarvon in February 1915. The battalion, whose official title was the 11th Battalion of the East Lancashire Regiment, remained at Caernarvon until May, when it was transferred to Penkridge Camp, near Rugeley in Staffordshire. Two more moves took place, firstly to Ripon and then to Salisbury, before the Accrington Pals received orders to leave for Egypt in December 1915. Their mission in Egypt was to fight the Turks and guard the Suez Canal, but their time there was short and they were posted to France in February 1916.

The commanders of the British and French armies had, by this time, already decided to launch a major offensive in the Somme area in the summer of that year. Initially, this was due to be a joint attack, but severe French losses at Verdun necessitated a change of plan and the Battle of the Somme became a mainly British operation: one in which many Pals battalions would partake.

The Accrington Pals were part of the assault on a hilltop fortress at Serre. Despite a week-long bombardment prior to July 1st, the attacking troops came up against heavy machine-gun fire on the first day of of the battle. Only a handful of men reached the enemy front-line trench and they were soon forced to retreat due to a lack of reinforcements. Of the 720 Accrington Pals who began the attack, only 136 were left when the battalion was relieved. The devastation of the Accrington Pals had taken less than half an hour.

The initial newspaper reports in Accrington stated that the battle was going well and that primary objectives had been taken. These optimistic accounts were soon replaced by growing lists of casualties and, as the reality became clear, the folly of sending men from the same area into battle together soon began to be evident. Almost every family felt the effects and the town, like many others, went into mourning for its lost sons.

Later, the battalion was brought back up to strength again and saw further service during the First World War before being disbanded in 1919. However, the comradeship which had epitomised the ethos of the Pals Battalions was lost forever, along with the men who had answered their country's call.

THE BATTLE OF THE SOMME

In late 1915, the Allies held a conference at Chantilly to the north of Paris. Here they decided that in 1916, major assaults would be made on all fronts, in an attempt to finally break down the German army. As part of this objective it was agreed that the French and British would combine on the Western Front in a major offensive at the point where their two armies met - the River Somme. The Commander in Chief of the British Army, General Sir Douglas Haig, preferred the idea of attacking further to the north, in Flanders, but was overruled by his opposite number in the French army, General Joseph Joffre. The French commander saw the forthcoming battle as one of attrition: his aim being to wear down the German army, rather than worry about making any significant territorial gains.

In February 1916, while Haig and Joffre were still planning the anticipated attack, the Germans launched a massive offensive at Verdun. The German intention here was similar to Joffre's at the Somme - to wear down the French army, or as the German Chief of Staff, Erich von Falkenhayn is alleged to have put it, to "bleed France white". Falkenhayn had chosen to attack at Verdun because he believed that the French would defend this historic town to the last man, rather than cede it to the Germans. As French losses began to mount, Joffre demanded that the launch date for the Battle of the Somme should be brought forward from 1st August to 1st July 1916 in order to divert German resources from Verdun. In addition it was decided that the Battle of the Somme would have to become a predominantly British affair, with the French only participating in the south of the region. Joffre's preoccupation with defending Verdun meant that Haig now assumed responsibility for the planning of the Battle of the Somme.

Haig decided that the Fourth Army, under General Rawlinson, should lead the attack, although the two men initially disagreed as to the methods which should be employed. Haig favoured a speedy assault with little preliminary bombardment to maximise the element of surprise. Once the infantry had broken through, he intended to use his beloved cavalry to charge the German forces and turn the war back into a mobile one, rather than the stalemate it had become. Rawlinson, on the other hand, was an infantry man and preferred a more cautious approach, with a long bombardment followed by an infantry attack over a wider front, with a 'creeping barrage' being laid down by the artillery to protect the advancing troops. The two sides were never fully reconciled although Haig was forced to concede that a prolonged artillery attack was necessary in order to break down the strong German fortifications.

On 24th June the bombardment began, and continued until 1st July. The Germans had, however, built extremely strong defences and had occupied them for many months, thus ensuring that while the bombardment caused them great hardship, they survived - as did their front line. At 7.28am on 1st July, 17 mines were detonated along the front. Unfortunately, one of these mines exploded eight minutes earlier, giving the Germans advance notice of the impending attack. The men were ordered to go over the top at 7.30am and advance across No Man's Land at a walking pace. There were many reasons for this, including the general's misguided belief that the Germans and their defences would already have been destroyed by the artillery bombardment and that the men would find nothing but abandoned trenches awaiting them. In addition, Rawlinson was concerned that the New Army which formed the backbone of his force might begin to straggle once out in the open. In order for the 'creeping barrage' to work, the infantry must be kept together, rather than wandering off and risking being caught up in their own artillery fire.

Unfortunately, the barrage had failed in its aim of decimating the German defences and once the mines had exploded and the bombardment ceased, the German soldiers came out of their reinforced bunkers to man their machine guns. At the same time, the German artillery opened fire on No-Man's Land. The advancing British troops were an easy target, especially as much of the German barbed wire remained intact. While the bombardment may have failed to destroy its target, both it and the ensuing German artillery fire succeeded in severing the communication lines which had been laid down previously. This meant that the Generals behind the lines remained largely ignorant of what was taking place. Initial reports which filtered back to Headquarters were optimistic and orders were then issued which did not reflect the genuine requirements at the front. Reserves were sent to the wrong places and were, themselves, wiped out.

The date of July 1st 1916 is the bloodiest in British military history, and almost 60,000 men were either killed, wounded or reported missing on that day alone. Most of the men who went over the top that morning were the enthusiastic patriots of Kitchener's volunteer army, many of them from the newly formed Pals battalions. The men of the original British Expeditionary Force had effectively been wiped out in previous battles and, for many of the new recruits, the Somme was to be their first, and last, taste of battle.

The Battle of the Somme continued, despite these losses, and in one sense, one of Joffre's goals was achieved. The Germans were forced to transfer some troops and munitions from Verdun, which gave the French a welcome respite and allowed them to regain some control in that area.

By August, Haig had accepted that his hoped-for breakthrough was unlikely and the British concentrated on smaller actions while continuing to prepare for another 'big push'. This began on 15th

September and is remembered mainly as the battle in which tanks made their debut. Haig had been a keen observer of the development of this new technology, but their impact was disappointing. Numbers were few, they were mechanically unreliable and in the cloying mud of the Somme, those that did not break down soon became stuck. The main achievement of the tank was to frighten the opposition. During this attack, despite the failure of the tanks, gains were made and it was deemed to have been a success, although once again, there was no great breakthrough.

As autumn approached, Haig continued to launch new offensives, hoping to break the German lines. However, the weather now worsened, turning the battlefield into a bog. Eventually the fighting in this area ceased near the end of November, leaving both sides to count the cost. Total Allied casualties during the battle were in excess of 600,000, with Germany losing roughly the same amount, although the figures were difficult to confirm. Germany's army had, until that time, been made up of regular soldiers, but would in future be compiled of conscripts and volunteers which, to a certain extent, made both sides more equal from then on.

Many historians have argued that Haig should bear responsibility for the massive losses incurred in the Battle of the Somme: that he should have ceased the attack once the level of casualties became clear. Others point out that he was bound by many restrictions, such as the political requirement to adhere to the wishes of the French Army; outdated war tactics and the need to fight a totally different type of war. These two opposing sides remain intransigent, each using selective reasoning and choosing to either ignore or dismiss any alternative to their own viewpoint.

What remains as an indisputable fact is that the Battle of the Somme and, in particular, its opening day, would become firmly etched in the mind of the British public, as the day when innocence was lost.

THEMES

SACRIFICE

This, together with the waste and futility of the conflict is a common theme in the literature of the First World War. *The Accrington Pals*, being a play about the decimation of a town and its people, features it perhaps more strongly than most. The fact that the men all come from the same place and many of them either live close together or work in the same places, heightens the sense of loss and sacrifice as the audience comes to understand the consequences of this method of recruiting when so many men are lost. It is not just the men who are called upon to make the 'ultimate sacrifice', but the whole town - including the women and children - whose lives will never be the same again.

The central male character, Tom Hackford, is portrayed as a very young, idealistic, romantic man, who has a bright future and everything to live for. Tom's death symbolises the waste of the war and the indiscriminate nature of death.

By using an idealist as a central character, Peter Whelan is forcing the audience to question what might have been. If Tom had survived, for example, would he have gone into politics and become a leader of men. Would he have fulfilled all of his ambitions and did his sacrifice prove to be worthwhile. These are questions which remain unanswered because Tom has taken the decision to answer his nation's call and do his duty, and in doing so has sacrificed his life, and his hopes for the future.

Of all the characters in the play, the only one who senses the futility of the war is May. She realises that Tom might be throwing away his life and his ambitions and fails to understand the sense of duty which has driven him to enlist. Strangely, May also represents the antithesis of the idea of futility, as she sees the conditions brought about by the war as a good way to earn more money and enhance her business prospects.

A good example of the futile nature of the war can be seen in Ralph's letter to Eva at the beginning of Act Two. This scene follows Tom and May's argument and May's angry conversation with CSM Rivers, who has been pointing out the bravery of the men. In his letter, Ralph seems much less cheerful than normal. This may be because of his guilt over having slept with prostitutes, but there is also a sense of boredom and desperation. He speaks of waiting and being moved about a lot - all to no purpose. However, now he knows that there is a big battle ahead, he is unsure how he will face up to what he knows he must do. He also relates the conditions in the trenches and in No Man's Lane, indicating that this ground has been fought over before, but to no avail as the Pals are about to fight there again.

These themes are undercurrents which run throughout the play and which draw in the audience. This is made possible by the use of dramatic irony. The audience know that the first day of the Battle of the Somme cost many thousands of lives, but they also know that little ground was gained by these deaths and that the war dragged on for more than two years following the beginning of the attack which many characters in the play anticipate will be the final 'big push'. Many in the audience would also be familiar with the plight of the Pals battalions during that time. The characters are portrayed, quite accurately, as ignorant of their fate, which enhances the sense of a pointless sacrifice for the audience.

The scenes where the women discover the severity of the casualties also serve to highlight this theme. The initial estimate of seven survivors stuns the women and even the revised number quoted by CSM Rivers means that there would be hardly a single house in the town that remained unaffected by these catastrophic and costly losses.

Pals relaxing at Rugeley Camp. (Image Ref: WT55-4)
Image courtesy of William Turner Collection, Lancashire County Library and Information Service

CHANGING TIMES

The years immediately before and after the First World War saw great changes in society, class, status and attitudes. One of the most obvious of these was the change in the role of women. In *The Accrington Pals*, the women all have strong, forceful characters, most of them work in the mill and have done for many years. Until the war, they did not expect their lives to consist of anything but mill-work, marriage and children. With the war came new opportunities to undertake a different type of work, to travel more and to improve themselves.

May provides a good example of a strong, independent woman. She does not feel the need to have a man in her life and is happy to put all of her efforts into enhancing her business opportunities. She obviously feels that women are not as well treated as they should be, as she points out to Eva that the women are not as well paid as the men would be. Her interpretation of this is that if women continue to rely on men, they will always find themselves taking second place. May's fierce independence and distrust of others is behind these sentiments, but the facts are nonetheless true. Bertha's treatment on the trams provides another example of this inequality. Bertha has given up her job at the mill and gone to work on the trams. Once there, however, she discovers that the men feel threatened by the presence of women in their workplace. The women are not allowed into the rest room during their breaks and they are not paid as much as the men because they are, supposedly, not strong enough to do their work without assistance. This demonstrates the adjustments that both men and women were having to make and also how their attitudes varied. Eva, for example, seems to feel that her role is unimportant because she does not have to risk her life. Sarah, on the other hand, points out that the women working in the munitions factories are working in dangerous and unhealthy conditions.

The war placed women in a difficult social position. Their labour was required and, as the war progressed, it became a necessity, yet 'convention' still expected them to behave with due decorum. This was a new and awkward role for women, as their new-found independence gave them more freedom, but there were still restrictions on what was deemed to be acceptable behaviour. This gender confusion was enhanced by government propaganda and newspaper reports which portrayed men as heroes, going to war to protect their women from the German onslaught. Regardless of the accuracy of this statement, it is easy to see why both men and women found their new roles unclear. Men had traditionally been the bread-winners, but were now having to hand this role over to the women, who in turn became more independent, while being told that they still needed 'protecting'.

Another aspect of life and society that changed during the war was the attitude towards sex. In *The Accrington Pals*, this is best represented by May and Eva. May seems distant and inexperienced in her relationship with Tom, but as the war progresses, she mellows and softens towards him, even to the extent of contemplating suggesting that he sleep with her while on leave. This behaviour is out of character for May, but she has realised that her feelings for Tom are more intense than she had previously thought.

While, for May, an argument with Tom leaves this matter unsettled, Eva has already had sex with Ralph. Like many of her contemporaries, she is not prepared to wait for marriage. Sarah, for example, expresses her anger that the war didn't begin three years earlier, thus avoiding her having a child and getting married. Note, she doesn't say that she got married and had a child. Initially, sensing May's disapproval, Eva tries to keep the extent of her relationship with Ralph a secret, but eventually decides that she must be honest and reveals the truth. Although she tries to appear understanding, it is clear that May finds Eva and Ralph's situation difficult to accept.

Despite obvious encouragement from Tom, May continues to believe in self-control.

Although there had always been men and women who didn't believe in the convention of waiting for marriage before having sexual intercourse, there was a marked increase during the First World War. Many reflected, like Eva, that to wait for an event that might never happen was pointless.

The war changed lives in other ways too. The Trade Union movement, which was still in its infancy, found many new followers, as represented by the character of Tom. He advocates the power of the collective voice and this reflects real changes that were occurring in social and political spheres. His friends find his attitude difficult to understand. To them his ideas seem unrealistic, as they have always accepted their lot in life. Linked to these changes was the blurring between different classes in society. In *The Accrington Pals*, May, who is always striving for a better social position, associates with the ladies of Peel Park, admiring their houses and clothes. She clearly aspires to be respected by them, while the other girls seem to think May has developed ideas above her station and is, in fact, demeaning herself. Sarah resents the upper-class ladies who become nurses - and the publicity which they seem to gain, while others, like Sarah, are working too.

RELATIONSHIPS

The Accrington Pals, being primarily a play about people, features their relationships and how their involvement in the war has great consequences. The main relationship in this play is between Tom Hackford and May Hassal. Having known each other for a few years, their friendship is already established. The most immediate effect of the war on their relationship is Tom's enlistment in the Pals battalion. May is unhappy at his going, although the reason for this is unclear. She seems to feel responsible for him, but in her own way, she also loves him. In addition, he is of great use to her in running the stall. Although her attempts to get CSM Rivers to release Tom from his commitment are unsuccessful, she resents his decision to join up. Tom's feelings for May are more clear. His affection for her increases throughout the play, although they are destined to be divided. Tom develops a deep sense of duty and despite the fact that he momentarily offers to remain with May, one instinctively knows that he will be go, because he must.

Tom and May's relationship is awkward, partly because of the age difference between them, but mainly because they have such different views and opinions. Their politics and social outlooks are poles apart. Tom dreams of a society in which people are treated equally and valued by others for their individual skills and abilities; May, on the other hand, firmly believes in the power of the individual and that men and women can only prosper through their own efforts. Tom's ideals seem unrealistic to May, although she can appreciate that he has his own life a head of him and appears to believe that he is throwing away his future by enlisting.

Ralph and Eva have only been seeing each other for a few months. Theirs is a more stereotypical relationship, with Eva worrying that Ralph will forget all about her. She feels unsure about her future once he has gone. Ralph, on the other hand, cheats on Eva, sleeping with prostitutes while in France. Although he feels guilty about this, one senses that he misses the physical side of their relationship more than anything else.

Another stereotypical couple can be seen in Annie and Arthur Boggis. Annie seems to rule their household with a rod of iron and has barely a good word to say about either her husband or her son. Once the pigeon appears and Annie believes Arthur to be dead, she falls apart, becoming hysterical and clinging to Reggie for support. This seems a strange reaction from someone who had appeared not to care a great deal about her husband and there could be more than one explanation for this. It may be that her behaviour prior to Arthur's death was a fabrication and, although she may not have loved him greatly, it is perfectly possible that she did care for him, but found it necessary, for some reason, to pretend otherwise. This may have been because she preferred her neighbours to see her as a hard character, with no feelings for others. Alternatively, an explanation for her breakdown could be her concern for herself and Reggie now that Arthur is dead. They are a poor family and the loss of her husband, even though she and Reggie work, would have a huge impact on their finances and their future.

Another relationship which bears some scrutiny is that between May and Eva. Despite a faltering beginning, caused by Tom neglecting to mention Eva's arrival, the two women soon form a friendship. May has a reputation among her neighbours for her high expectations and desire to better herself. Eva, being fair-minded, refuses to judge her new friend, showing loyalty towards May, who has given her a job and a roof over her head. She remains grateful to May, even when the older woman asks her to perform tasks which she is really unwilling to undertake, such as singing at the charity concert. May clearly trusts Eva and offers to make her a partner in her new business venture. Eva's scepticism about May's motives demonstrates her ability to understand May's real feelings, as she believes that May really hopes that Eva's presence will entice Ralph and, therefore, Tom to join the two women. Although May denies this accusation, it is clear that Eva has offended May and this episode marks the beginning of the end of their close friendship. Despite this, the audience know that May's feelings for Tom are stronger than she will admit and it is possible that she becomes angry with Eva because the younger girl has managed to see through May's defences.

COMPARISONS

EFFECTS OF THE WAR

In common with a great deal of other literature about the First World War, *The Accrington Pals* demonstrates how people reacted in different ways to various events during the war. In most cases, these reactions reflect the impact of the war on each individual, rather than its effects on the general population. May, for example, is torn between anger at Tom for enlisting and taking advantage of her newly discovered business opportunities. Tom, on the other hand, initially sees it as his duty to enlist and, once in the army, he is impressed by the efficiency and methods employed.

Unlike much of the other literature of the First World War, the effects of the war in *The Accrington Pals* are shown from the perspective of those left behind. This is mainly because of the unique nature of the Pals' involvement in the war and the realisation that such high casualties would have a profound impact on the areas involved. *The Return of the Soldier* by Rebecca West is another 'home-front' piece. In this novel, the hero, Chris Baldry has lost his memory and returns to his home still believing that he is in a relationship with his first love Margaret. He has no memory of his wife Kitty. The dilemma which faces these two women, and Chris's cousin Jenny is whether to return Chris to 'normal' and let him go back to the dangers of the war, or to keep him safe at home, living a false life. No such problems exist in the lives of the women in *The Accrington Pals*: their concerns are for how they will exist without their men. These two pieces go to demonstrate that the impact of the war on the individuals at home depended entirely upon their direct involvement, their class, their social and financial status and their relationship with the person they have lost.

In *The Accrington Pals*, as the war progresses, the people at home still continue to hold out hopes that the latest 'big push' will be the one to end the conflict. This portrayal of home-front complacency and its effects of giving unrealistically high-hopes, is the sort of reaction which angered many serving soldiers, especially some of the poets. Siegfried Sassoon was probably the most vociferous of these and frequently wrote poems which expressed his feelings of injustice and bitterness towards those at home, who continued to believe the 'lies'. Among these are *Glory of Women, Does it Matter?* and *Suicide in the Trenches*, all of which demonstrate the difference between the reality of the soldier's life and experiences and the portrayal of those experiences at home.

Eventually, some of the characters are seen to face up to the death of a loved-one and the audience witnesses the effect that this has upon their lives and personalities. The scale of losses in *The Accrington Pals* makes the impact of the deaths of the men much more forceful. The women initially believe that only seven men have survived, so all must face the stark reality of loss. However, their new-found independence makes them question the newspaper reports and they march on the town hall to discover the truth. The need for those at home to discover the truth about the men they have lost was a common reality. Many families would write to senior officers and the war office, desperate for news of loved-ones, or to discover the real facts behind a death. An example of this can be seen in *Strange Meeting* by Susan Hill, when David Barton's mother writes to John Hilliard, desperate for news of her son. All too often the information which families were able to glean was sketchy or incomplete. In fact, Rudyard Kipling, whose son John was killed on 27th September 1915 at the Battle of Loos, spent the rest of his life trying to discover the events which had led up to his son's death and the whereabouts of his body.

PORTRAYAL OF WOMEN

Much of the literature of the First World War leaves out the role of women altogether. In other pieces, women are portrayed less flatteringly than their male counterparts. This is not the case in *The Accrington Pals*. May, for example, while always independently seeking to better herself and leave the slums behind her, is also seen to be quietly kind-hearted. This 'roundness' of character can also be seen in Sarah Lumb, the central female character in Pat Barker's novel *Regeneration*. Sarah has a working-class background, works in a munitions factory and is fiercely independent. Her character, like many of those in *The Accrington Pals*, reflects the changes women were undergoing in the course of the war: active participation in the war effort, rather than a subservient role in society. At the same time, however, Sarah demonstrates her feelings of injustice towards the conflict. When she speaks of her dead boyfriend, she is angry that it was British gas which killed him. Equally, when she visits the hospital, she resents the maimed men being hidden away from the public - believing that a nation which expects its young men to give so much, should at least have the decency to face the consequences.

All of the female characters in *The Accrington Pals* have strong personalities, they say what they think and are not necessarily prepared to believe everything they are told. Their roles change as the war progresses and this is reflected by most of the female characters taking on additional or different work to help in the war effort. The changing role of working women during the First World War is also portrayed in Jessie Pope's poem *War Girls*, in which she describes the various tasks undertaken by women and their loyalty to both their men and their country. As with most of her work, Pope's portrayal is idealistic, although there is an element of reality in this poem, as shown in *The Accrington Pals*. The suggestion in both of these pieces is that, regardless of what happens to their men, the role of women in society has changed.

Many of the other women, with the obvious exception of Eva, are not sorry to see their men go and fight and seem to think it only right that they should have joined up. Bertha's reaction to the attentions of a young man who has failed his medical examination are noteworthy. Although he cannot help his illness, Bertha seems to think there would be an element of shame attached to marrying, or even loving him. This attitude is also reflected in the play *Oh What a Lovely War*, where women are portrayed as goading men into enlisting and showing contempt for those who refuse. This latter play, however, provides a stereotypical account of the First World War, as seen from the 1960s. *The Accrington Pals* would seem, therefore, to give a more realistic portrayal, showing many different reactions, based as much on individual personalities and relationships as on a general train of thought.

The women in *The Accrington Pals* are shown to be much more involved in the war effort and the lives of their menfolk than many other female characters in First World War literature. These women, with a few exceptions, show their emotions and are not afraid of demonstrating their feelings for others. Many authors frequently portray women as unfeeling or aloof from the circumstances which are unravelling around them. Kitty in *The Return of the Soldier* by Rebecca West is shown to be a selfish, uncaring woman who refuses to let the war have any impact on her lifestyle or existence. When her husband returns to her unaware, due to amnesia, that they are even married, her sole concern is how this event will impact on her life and social status. She shows no concern for her husband's future wellbeing, but is merely anxious to regain her pre-war life. Equally, the character of Constance Hilliard in Susan Hill's *Strange Meeting* is emotionally constrained, never revealing her feelings to her son, despite the losses he suffers during the war. She is a woman who is incapable of showing emotion, keeping her feelings, if she has any, firmly to herself. It could be argued, however, that these differences are as much to do with class and social status as anything else. Both Kitty and Constance are upper-class ladies, who have probably been raised to believe that it is a weakness to show one's feelings. The women in *The Accrington Pals* have no such scruples - how their demonstrations of emotion are perceived is unimportant to them.

FAITH

Faith, including the loss of it, is a common theme in First World War literature, with many authors examining the role of religious beliefs during the conflict. This can take the form of characters discovering, maintaining or losing their belief in God. A change of beliefs at such a time is hardly surprising or unreasonable. The vast majority of soldiers were being placed in situations they had never experienced before and some of the events they witnessed were enough to make anyone question their previously held convictions. For some, the prospect of their own impending death made them more ready to turn to God for guidance, while others, who may previously have held strong beliefs, began to question God's role in the carnage they were enduring.

In *The Accrington Pals*, Arthur Boggis is clearly a religious man and, in his very first appearance, the conversation rapidly turns to God. In fact, his speeches always revolve around his beliefs. Prior to his departure, he says a prayer to the assembled company. The others join in, except Tom, who seems to follow no religion. Arthur's letter to his friend Jack explains his feelings about the war and his belief that he is doing God's work. He asserts that it is man's failure to live by God's laws that have brought about the conflict and that this is His way of purifying the world of its sins. However, this letter is written while Arthur is still in training and once he is in the trenches, his outlook changes. When CSM Rivers suggests that Arthur say a prayer before they go over-the-top, Arthur's response is to sarcastically ask God if he finds their situation pleasing. His experiences and the sights he has witness have clearly affected his beliefs. This change of heart is confirmed by CSM Rivers when he tells May that Arthur had denied his God before he died. In common with others, Arthur's experiences have made him question how his God could allow such atrocities to take place: how He could allow such suffering.

This is echoed in *Birdsong* by Sebastian Faulks. In this novel, the character Jack Firebrace, like Arthur Boggis, has a long-standing and deep-rooted belief in God. As the story progresses, Jack's faith is continually tested. Firstly his young son becomes seriously ill and then, despite Jack's prayers, the boy dies. Although some might believe, at such a time, that they had been let down by their God, Jack's faith remains intact. In fact, he writes to his grieving wife at home and tells her that they should be grateful to God for allowing them the opportunity of knowing their wonderful son. However, on 1st July 1916, everything changes. Jack, as a tunneller is not one of the soldiers going over-the-top. Instead he and his friend, together with the Padré stand behind the lines, and from their vantage point, they witness the carnage of the first day of the Battle of the Somme. The massacre unfolding before them leaves these men altered: Arthur Shaw, Jack's friend - a strong, burly miner, cries like a baby; the Padré, Horrocks, throws away his silver cross in disgust, unable to believe the sights he is witnessing. Jack, meanwhile, knows and silently accepts that his belief in God has gone forever.

A QUESTION OF COMPARISONS

Many students have to make direct comparisons between two particular texts, demonstrating the author's treatment of a specific topic. Where this is dealt with as coursework, some examination boards allow that the student may be permitted to choose the texts for themselves. To that end, we have included a list of possible topics and suggested texts which, in our opinion, provide suitable material for such essays, assuming that *The Accrington Pals* will be one of the texts involved. What follows below is not a series of 'answers' because in this situation, it is for each student to decide what to include and how they wish to study each piece in question. Instead, this section is meant to whet the appetite: to give students a point from which to start in making their own comparisons.

THE CHANGING ROLE OF WOMEN

Quite often in the literature of the First World War, the role of women is minimalised, or even non-existent. *The Accrington Pals* is a notable exception to this, providing ample examples of the way in which women were forced to change their lives as a result of the conflict.

Using The Accrington Pals and Regeneration

The women in both of these pieces are working-class, independent and strong. Students could choose to focus either on the general role of women as portrayed in these two works, or take particular characters and study their personalities and lives more closely.

For example, although Sarah Lumb in *Regeneration* and May Hassal in *The Accrington Pals* both work, Sarah works in a munitions factory, aware that she has a responsibility to 'do her bit' for the war effort.

May, on the other hand, runs her own business and is always looking for ways to improve both it and herself. However, Sarah's outlook is not entirely selfless as she chose to work in the munitions factory rather than be a servant - the pay is better, but also she resents the idea of being subservient. Both women have adapted well to their situations: May's strong independence stands her in good stead, while Sarah's quick mind and forceful character ensure that nobody will get the better of her. Both Sarah and May are slow to show their emotions - neither one really prepared to commit themselves to the men who claim to love them.

Students who choose to focus on the general representation of the role of women within these pieces could look at the language which both authors have used. The women in both pieces often meet together outside of their workplaces. Their discussions focus on the men in their lives; their working conditions; occasionally the war and their friendships with each other. Their language is invariably coarse or masculine, showing their down-to-earth nature.

PORTRAYAL OF FRIENDSHIPS IN WAR

Many pieces of First World War literature, both poetry and prose, look at the friendships formed during the war. Usually, these friendships concern men who meet as a consequence of the war, but there is no reason why students could not choose to compare these friendships with those formed by the women left behind.

Using The Accrington Pals and Journey's End

The friendships in The Accrington Pals - with the exception of that between Tom and Ralph - are between women. They all work or live in close proximity and share the similar fate of having their menfolk go off to fight in the war. This circumstance brings them all much closer together, ensuring a common bond and a strength of friendship which is, probably, new to these women. Although their lives are less harsh or dangerous than the men's, they still have the daily hardships of working-class life to contend with - except that now they are alone. They also have to deal with their fears about their men not returning and what will happen to them in that event. The women have differing opinions on many matters, such as whether or not the men should have joined up in the first place, but the audience is left with the impression that, ultimately, these women will remain bound together in their grief and hardship.

Journey's End, on the other hand, is about a group of soldiers, thrown together in a dug-out in the spring of 1918. These men know that an attack is about to take place and that there is every chance that they will not all survive. In the short time that the audience spends with them, it becomes clear that these men have become like a close-knit family unit. They must remain loyal to each other in order to fight at their best. They also understand that their relationships with one another are probably the strongest that they will experience in their lives.

Students who choose to study these two plays in this way should pay attention to the social class of the two sets of people involved: *Journey's End* concerns officers - most of whom are upper or middle class; *The Accrington Pals* has a working class setting. This means that the characters will react to their situations differently, but it is interesting to note that both sets of people show an element of reserve in their emotional reactions.

NOT ABOUT HEROES
BY STEPHEN MACDONALD

INTRODUCTION

First performed in 1982, this is probably one of the most underrated First World War plays. It details the friendship between Wilfred Owen and Siegfried Sassoon, from their initial meeting at Craiglockhart, to Owen's death.

Told from Sassoon's perspective, in a series of flashbacks, it is a humourous, tragic and above all, moving account of this friendship and is based on diary entries and extracts from letters and autobiographies, giving it a sense of authenticity.

The two things which strike one most are the strength of feelings in this unlikely friendship between two men from very different backgrounds, and the realisation of what was lost when Wilfred Owen failed to return from France.

Publicity still from production of *Not About Heroes* - Performed at
the Barons Court Theatre 2005, directed by Ian Flintoff
Siegfried Sassoon (Dov Citron) and Wilfred Owen (Martin Scully)
Image courtesy of MAD House Plays

SYNOPSIS

ACT ONE

While sitting in his study on November 3rd 1932, Siegfried Sassoon remembers Wilfred Owen's departure from Craiglockhart, fifteen years earlier.

4th November 1917
Owen and Sassoon meet up just prior to Owen's departure and Sassoon gives his young friend a volume of poems which he hopes Owen will find amusing. They briefly argue about Owen's decision to leave Craiglockhart and Sassoon's belief that the younger man is not yet fit enough to return to duty. They discuss the volume of poetry, which contains some unusual and occasionally incomprehensible verses. Owen is grateful to Sassoon, but unsure how to express himself and they briefly reminisce about their first meeting, just a couple of months earlier. Sassoon gives Owen an envelope before they embrace, after which Owen gives Sassoon a letter. Their parting is highly charged and emotional and, although both men attempt to maintain an air of bravado, their fear of losing one another is obvious.

Returning to 1932, Sassoon re-reads some notes he had been making about Owen, recalling that, at the time of his departure, Owen had just one year left to live. He remembers their dependence on each other at the time and re-reads the letter which Owen had given him at their last meeting. Owen appears to Sassoon and reads an extract from his poem 'Strange Meeting', which makes Sassoon recall their first meeting at Craiglockhart. Owen is revealed as he had been in June 1917: a nervous, lonely isolated young man. He remained thus until he bought a copy of 'The Old Huntsman' and read Sassoon's work for the first time. In a letter to his mother, he speaks of how much these poems have

impressed him and reveals his knowledge of Sassoon's military
background. Sassoon himself recalls the consequences of his 'Declaration'
against the war: the authorities' decision to have him sent to
Craiglockhart. In another letter to his mother, Owen reveals his delight at
Sassoon's arrival and his intention of asking the revered poet to
autograph several copies of 'The Old Huntsman'.

August 1917
Owen, armed with his copies of 'The Old Huntsman', timidly knocks
at Sassoon's door and receives an abrupt invitation to enter.
Sassoon is gruff and unwelcoming and Owen hesitates in his
mission. Eventually, they begin to talk, discussing poetry, until
Sassoon's curiosity gets the better of him and he is forced to ask
why this stranger is walking about the hospital carrying copies of
his book. He graciously consents to autographing the books, which
Owen hands to him, together with a list of names. Sassoon re-reads
some of his early poems and finds it hard to believe that he could
have written them. Upon seeing the poem 'To My Brother', Owen
hesitatingly asks when Sassoon's brother had been killed. Sassoon
recalls Gallipoli - his brother's final resting place and the mood,
momentarily becomes sombre. In an effort to lighten the tone,
Sassoon makes a joke about Owen's colonel - little realising how
sensitive Owen is about this subject. Owen is flustered and begins
to stammer. Sassoon is angry with himself for upsetting the younger
officer. He begins signing the books and is surprised that one of
them is for Owen's mother, Susan. He fears that some of his poems
might be a little too realistic for her although Owen assures him
that he has already revealed the war's horrors in his letters.
Sassoon is surprised that Susan Owen is interested in the truth: his
experience of those at home is that they do not really *want* to
understand. They both believe that the men are being slaughtered
simply because no-one cares enough to stop the fighting. Owen
asks Sassoon to help him write poetry that reveals the truth and
recites Sassoon's poem 'The Death Bed' to prove the point that

Sassoon writes with great feeling for those who are suffering. The beauty of this poem forces Sassoon to reluctantly concede that he might have written something worthwhile. Eventually, Sassoon reaches the final book, but has no more names on the list - this one is for Owen. Sassoon realises then that he is unaware of his young visitor's name. Owen informs him and Sassoon obliges by completing his task before Owen leaves.

Sassoon recalls his feelings after this first meeting: his desire to see Owen again and his own shyness in Owen's presence.

A few days later, armed with manuscripts, Owen pays another visit to Sassoon, who he finds immersed in a letter from H G Wells. He asks Sassoon to look at some of his poems. Initially, however, Sassoon is critical of his style - especially in his older pieces - and Owen is disappointed. Later, when Sassoon reads 'The Next War' he is more impressed and asks Owen if he has written anything similar. Owen reluctantly reads some excerpts from 'Exposure' - a poem he has been working on. Sassoon is even more impressed and offers to speak to potential publishers. Owen's gratitude for this attention is clear in his letters to his mother and, over the coming weeks the two men meet every day as Owen continues to write.

Owen, who is the editor of the hospital journal 'The Hydra', asks Sassoon for a poem to be published in the next issue. Sassoon will only agree to this if Owen puts in one of his own. This prospect makes Owen very self-conscious and nervous, but Sassoon remains adamant and eventually Owen relents and prints one of his own pieces. Sassoon introduces Owen to Robert Graves to whom he shows some of Owen's work. Graves is impressed by 'Disabled' and writes to Owen about it, deciding that although the poem begins well enough, its qualities tail off towards the end. Owen takes this criticism to heart and Sassoon attempts, once again, to bolster his confidence.

During October, Sassoon hears news from Passchendaele and finds Owen, eager to discuss whether his young friend intends to return to the front. He tells Owen all of the shocking details he has heard, hoping to dissuade him from going back. Owen, however, is concerned that the messages in his poetry are less valued or convincing because, unlike Sassoon, he has not yet proved his own courage. Sassoon tries, unsuccessfully, to reassure Owen that bravery is over-rated, that to go back and face death is not necessary. Owen remains unconvinced, even when Sassoon reveals that he feels a fraud for remaining safely at Craiglockhart when there is nothing really wrong with him. As they sit together, Owen shows Sassoon the draft of 'Anthem for Doomed Youth' and Sassoon offers suggestions for minor alterations to the text. Once it is completed, Owen reads it aloud. Sassoon is deeply affected by this reading and profusely compliments an embarrassed Owen.

Sassoon then recalls, once again, Owen's departure and his gifts to Owen, which had included an introduction to Robert Ross. Owen writes to Sassoon, a letter full of abundant praise and declarations of his own feelings for Sassoon.

Main Points of Interest in Act One

IMPACT ON SASSOON
- The fact that fifteen years after their first meeting, Sassoon still seems haunted by Owen's death is clear from the very beginning of the play and shows the impact of this friendship.
- According to the play Sassoon seems to have kept much of the correspondence which passed between them, again demonstrating Owen's importance to him.

THE CHANGE IN OWEN
- Wilfred Owen begins the play as a nervous man, lacking in confidence, but once their friendship blossoms, he becomes more outgoing and develops a wry sense of humour.
- This change in Wilfred Owen's personality is shown through his poetry, which improves as time progresses, under Sassoon's guidance.

SASSOON'S INFLUENCE
- In terms of Owen's poetry, Sassoon has a clear influence, both on Owen's style and his growing belief in his own ability.
- Owen's hero worship of Sassoon also shows as he seems to want to emulate Sassoon's exploits: to prove that he too has courage.

ACT TWO

Sassoon remembers some of Owen's other letters, especially one in which he had described Robbie Ross introducing him to Arnold Bennett and H G Wells. He also gives details of the marriage between Robert Graves and Nancy Nicholson. While at the wedding, Owen had also been introduced to Max Beerbohm, William Heinemann and Edward Marsh. In a letter to Owen, Sassoon expresses his guilt about remaining safe at Craiglockhart, while others are still fighting and dying. He later writes again, telling Owen that he has been passed fit for General Service Overseas. Owen tells his mother in a letter of his fears for Sassoon, but also of his gratitude for the older man's attentions.

Looking back through an old diary, Sassoon remembers his journey back to France which resulted in him being shot in the head, the wound bringing a premature end to his war. Owen visits Sassoon in hospital in London...

During this visit, Sassoon appears dazed, but pleased to see Owen. He is also concerned that his head injury might make others think he is mad. Owen has brought one copy of Sassoons latest volume of poems, 'Counter Attack', which he wants Sassoon to sign for him. They discuss the reviews for this book, before Owen tells Sassoon the details of the people to whom he has been introduced by Robbie Ross. While reciting an excerpt from Owen's 'Mental Cases' Sassoon becomes deeply affected by a memory and his reaction troubles Owen. To help relieve the tension, Owen tells Sassoon that Heinemann has agreed to publish some of his poems. This helps Sassoon to recover his composure and he congratulates himself on having 'discovered' Owen.

Sensing that his friend is feeling a little better, Owen asks for help with a preface for the forthcoming publication, which he reads aloud. Sassoon is impressed. They talk about the possibility of Owen returning to France: he still has doubts about his own courage. He clearly admires Sassoon's bravery, but the older man explains that his actions stemmed from a desire for revenge over the death of his friend David. He begs Owen not to follow in his footsteps - not to long for death, simply to escape the horrors of life. Owen is kind and sympathetic towards Sassoon and, at his request, reads his poem 'Futility', changing the third line to reflect David's Welsh roots. Sassoon is touched by this and realises that Owen's poetry is truly great, as well as beginning to understand Owen's intense regard for himself.

Owen pushes Sassoon's wheelchair out into the hospital garden and here they talk about their respective families. Owen eventually succeeds in getting Sassoon to discuss his injury. It would seem that Sassoon and a Corporal named Davis had gone out on a raid and, while in No Man's Land, Sassoon had removed his tin helmet and stood up, whereupon he was shot in the head by a Sergeant from his own Company. After telling his story, Sassoon becomes very tired and Owen takes him back indoors. Sassoon is deeply troubled and Owen tries to comfort him before departing.

In a letter to his mother, Owen makes it clear that he has decided to go back to France. When Sassoon hears of this, he is devastated and blames himself for not preventing Owen's departure. Alone, Sassoon reflects on their correspondence and the changing direction of the war, as it would seem that the Allies are finally making some progress. Owen writes to Sassoon, explaining the numbness towards his surroundings that he has begun to experience. He also reveals that he has been recommended for the Military Cross. This medal is duly awarded. Owen believes that the end of the war may be in sight. Sassoon writes to Owen detailing a meeting between himself and Winston Churchill and revealing how he longs to be back in France - with Owen. Owen's next letter mentions a possible armistice.

Sassoon seems haunted by Owen and sadly recalls the events which led up to his death. Then he returns to his papers and, tearing them up, resolves to remember Owen's happiness, the joy of their time together and the immeasurable pleasure which Owen's brief presence brought into his life.

Not About Heroes - Performed at the Barons Court Theatre 2005, directed by Ian Flintoff
Siegfried Sassoon (Dov Citron) and Wilfred Owen (Martin Scully)
Image courtesy of MAD House Plays

Main Points of Interest in Act Two

OWEN'S REPUTATION GROWS

- Through Robbie Ross, Owen is introduced to many influential literary friends: this shows how far his confidence has grown since meeting Sassoon.
- Plans are being made to publish a volume of Owen's work.

FINAL PARTING

- Owen decides to return to France - against Sassoon's wishes, but once there he seems more at peace with himself and finally gets to prove himself.
- Owen's death clearly has a profound effect on Sassoon, but despite his sadness at losing his friend, Sassoon chooses to remember him positively.

Inscription on the tombstone of Siegfried Sassoon,
St Andrew's Church, Mells.
Image courtesy of S Lawrance

BIOGRAPHIES

Ordinarily, a study guide would include a section on character analysis. However, in the case of *Not About Heroes*, the characters are real people. As such, we have included below biographies of the personalities involved in the play and others who are merely mentioned, but whose background details might help students to understand their influence and involvement in the lives of the two main characters.

SIEGFRIED SASSOON

Siegfried Loraine Sassoon was born on 8th September 1886 at the family home of Weirleigh at Matfield in Kent. He was the middle of three sons of Alfred and Theresa Sassoon. Alfred was from a wealthy Jewish banking family, but had been disowned by his mother upon his marriage to Theresa, who was not of the Jewish faith. Theresa was a Thornycroft by birth, with an intelligent and artistic nature. She was a strong, independent woman and was very protective of her talented son. Alfred and Theresa separated when Siegfried was five years old and Alfred died four years later of tuberculosis.

Other than these episodes, Siegfried passed a happy and secure childhood, enjoying reading, music, nature and, of course, writing poetry. He was educated at Marlborough and then went on to Clare College, Cambridge, where he studied Law and History, but left without obtaining a degree.

Back at home in Kent, he led a "country squire's" existence of hunting, riding point-to-point races and playing cricket. It was during this time that he was introduced to Edmund Gosse, who became a great influence in Sassoon's early literary career. Siegfried sent Gosse some of his poems and the critic thought well enough of them to show them to Edward Marsh, who was, at that time, Editor of the *Georgian Poetry* anthologies. Marsh was impressed and he and Sassoon became friends. At Marsh's suggestion, Sassoon moved to London in March 1914 but, despite the obvious advantages of being in London's literary circle, he struggled to maintain his new lifestyle on his limited allowance.

Upon the outbreak of war, Sassoon put his financial worries behind him and immediately enlisted as a Trooper in the Sussex Yeomanry. Siegfried's poetry at this time reflected his limited experiences and included enthusiastic verse, such as *Absolution*. A bad fall while riding, however, left Siegfried with a broken arm. When he had recovered from this injury, he transferred to the infantry and was commissioned into the Royal Welch Fusiliers in May 1915.

After training, Siegfried left for France on 24 November 1915 and joined the First Battalion at Béthune. It was at this time that he met fellow poet and Royal Welch Fusilier, Robert Graves, with whom he shared an initially intense friendship, which became acrimonious in the late 1920's and early 1930's.

By now the war was becoming more personal for Siegfried. His younger brother, Hamo, was mortally wounded at Gallipoli and was buried at sea on 1st November 1915. Then on 18th March 1916, his close friend, Second Lieutenant David Thomas was shot in the throat while out with a wiring party, and died of his wound. David Thomas had been an object of great affection for Sassoon, who wrote very movingly of him in *The Last Meeting*.

These losses had a profound effect on Sassoon and the war became a personal crusade to avenge these deaths. He took to creeping about in front of the British wire, with reckless enthusiasm and soon earned the nickname "Mad Jack". In June his platoon was involved in a raid on Kiel Trench and his selfless actions in retrieving the dead and wounded from No Man's Land earned him the Military Cross. The citation read:

"Owing to his courage and determination, all killed and wounded were brought in".

Sassoon went on to take part in the Battle of the Somme, being recommended for another medal, following a bombing raid. In late July Siegfried became ill with trench fever and was sent home to convalesce. He spent some time with Robert Ross, who had been a close friend of Oscar Wilde. Ross, in turn, introduced Siegfried to Arnold Bennett and HG Wells. During this leave, Sassoon also spent some time with Robert Graves, both at Graves's parent's holiday home in Harlech and then at his own mother's house in Kent.

Sassoon returned to France in February 1917 but after just two days, was forced into hospital, suffering from German measles. Upon returning to the front, ten days later, he joined the Second Battalion of the Royal Welch Fusiliers and participated in the Second Battle of the Scarpe, during which he was wounded in the shoulder.

As the war progressed, Sassoon's poetry became more bitter, as he experienced more and more of the needless slaughter of his fellow men. The ultimate effect of this was the writing of his *Declaration*, in July 1917, which he undertook while convalescing from his shoulder wound in England. He was influenced, it must be said, by prominent pacifists, such as John Middleton Murry and Bertrand Russell. In his *Declaration*, Sassoon does not criticise the men who were fighting, or the conduct of the war, but questions the validity of the cause, which he claims has been altered by unimaginative politicians, whose insincerities are resulting in the sacrifices of so many young lives. This was a difficult time for Sassoon, who felt that he was living a double life - deceiving those who did not know about his intentions.

Sassoon's aim in making his *Declaration* had been the publicity of a court martial, regardless of its consequences, but this was averted by his friends, including Robert Graves and Edward Marsh. Once Sassoon had been convinced, by Graves, that the authorities would never court martial him, he accepted a medical board which, after emotional evidence given by Graves, declared that Sassoon was suffering from shell-shock. Sassoon, who had by now become so disillusioned that he had thrown his medal ribbon into the Mersey river, found himself at Craiglockhart War Hospital, in Edinburgh. The diagnosis of shell-shock was very probably one of convenience for the authorities, desperate to avoid the embarrassment of a courageous and decorated officer, publicly and defiantly opposing the continuation of the war.

Sassoon continued to write poetry throughout this time - some of it amongst his most powerful. During his time at Craiglockhart, Sassoon was treated by Dr W. H. R. Rivers, who came to have a great influence over him and the two men remained close friends until the doctor's death in 1922.

Another, more famous, meeting at this time, was with Wilfred Owen, who was also a patient at Craiglockhart. Sassoon encouraged Owen, in whom he could perceive a genuine and natural talent for writing poetry. While it would seem that Owen may have harboured strong feelings of hero-worship for Sassoon, it is much less clear how the older man felt. It may be that he was attracted to Owen, but had a natural reticence as well as a fear of discovery which ensured that he kept his emotions to himself.

Sassoon suffered from feelings of extreme guilt at being safe at home, while his men were fighting in France, and he made the difficult decision to return to France, although he refused to acknowledge that his *Declaration* had been a mistake. On 26th November 1917, he was passed fit for general service.

On 13th February 1918, Sassoon sailed from Southampton and,
following a long journey, arrived, not in France, but in Palestine.
After three months, in what Sassoon found to be an uncomfortably
hot climate, he was glad to be sent back to the Western Front.
Once settled, Sassoon's foolhardiness re-surfaced and after leading a
terrified corporal on a raid into No Man's Land, a euphoric Sassoon
removed his helmet and stood up in a shell-hole, only to be shot in
the head. He later discovered that he had been shot by one of his
own sergeants, who had mistaken him for an advancing German.
This wound, while not fatal, was serious enough to mean the end of
Sassoon's war and he was placed on indefinite sick leave and
eventually retired from the army on 12th March 1919.

After the war, Sassoon waited to hear from Owen and it was quite
a long time before he heard of the death of his young friend. In his
autobiography, *Siegfried's Journey*, he describes the void which
Owen's loss left in his life, while expressing his pleasure at the
growing recognition of Owen's work.

In the period immediately following the war, Sassoon met many
famous writers, including T.E. Lawrence (Lawrence of Arabia) and
Thomas Hardy, with whom he frequently visited. He also, briefly,
became literary editor of the *Daily Herald* and while there received
a privately printed volume of poems from Edmund Blunden and
through shared interests in poetry and cricket, the two became life-
long friends.

Sassoon, in 1928, began writing his autobiographies, initially as a
fictionalised account in *Memoirs of a Fox-hunting Man, Memoirs of an
Infantry Officer* and finally *Sherston's Progress*, which are collectively
known as *The Complete Memoirs of George Sherston*. He then
published the non-fiction versions, entitled *The Old Century and
Seven More Years, The Weald of Youth* and *Siegfried's Journey*. This is not
to say that he ceased writing poetry, but he felt a need to expunge
his memories and experiences of the war.

Sassoon's homosexuality, which had remained unfulfilled and dormant throughout the war, heightened and he embarked on several romantic adventures, particularly during his travels into Europe during the 1920's. One of his longest-running and probably most personally destructive relationships began in 1927, when he met Stephen Tennant, the younger brother of Edward 'Bim' Tennant - another war poet, who had died during the Battle of the Somme. There was a considerable age-gap between Tennant and Sassoon and, while he cared deeply for the younger man, Sassoon gradually began to feel that he was less important to Tennant than he would have liked.

Eventually, however, Sassoon tired of the fickle nature of these friendships not to mention the emotional turmoil in which he frequently found himself, which was occasionally so upsetting that it made him physically ill. In 1933, he met Hester Gatty, the daughter of a prominent barrister and the Chief Justice of Gibraltar. This was not the first woman to whom Sassoon had been attracted and within days he had decided that he wanted to marry her. Many of his friends seemed surprised at this action but on 18th December 1933, they were married. They chose to live in Wiltshire at Heytesbury House, where in October 1936 Hester and Siegfried had a son, named George.

However, despite his abiding and intense love for his son, Sassoon also craved solitude. Hester, on the other hand, was keen to share her husband's interests and activities. This fostered a great resentment on Sassoon's part and he excluded her whenever possible. Neither party was entirely blameless, although friends were apt to take sides and the couple separated in 1945. From then on Sassoon saw less of George than he would have liked, and for a while father and son were virtual strangers. In 1957, after much thought and reflection, Sassoon was received into the Roman Catholic Church. In making this decision, he was helped and advised by two friends: Ronald Knox, a prominent catholic and author and Katharine Asquith (widow of Raymond) who lived at Mells Manor in Somerset. While staying with Katharine, Sassoon had always been impressed by the sense of tranquility with which she managed to surround herself, despite having lost both her husband and brother - Edward Horner - during the First World War. Sassoon's conversion to Catholicism brought him a greater inner peace than he had ever experienced before.

From then on, Sassoon lived a quiet existence at Heytesbury House, despite bouts of ill health, and was reconciled to George who was present at his death on September 1st 1967. He is buried at St Andrew's Church at Mells in Somerset. This was Sassoon's choice of resting place as he wanted to be buried near to his friend, Ronald Knox. This church, like so many others, has many reminders of the First World War - including the original grave markers of Raymond Asquith and Edward Horner, which were brought back from France. An apt resting place indeed, surrounded by his beloved countryside, yet with the constant reminder of the war that changed his life.

St Andrew's Church,
Mells, Somerset
*Sassoon's grave is
bottom right with the
crosses.*

*Image courtesy of
S Lawrance*

WILFRED OWEN

Wilfred Edward Salter Owen was born on 18th March 1893 in Plas Wilmot near Oswestry in Shropshire. Until Wilfred was four the family lived in relative comfort in a house belonging to his grandfather, Edward Shaw - a former mayor of the city. Upon Shaw's death, it was discovered that he was virtually bankrupt and Wilfred and his family were forced to move to smaller lodgings in Birkenhead. Here they battled constant financial difficulties in attempting to maintain their previous lifestyle. This did not sit well with Wilfred's mother, Susan, who had an air of gentility and she determined that her beloved eldest son would, one day, restore the family fortune.

Wilfred had three younger siblings - a sister Mary and brothers Colin and Harold. He was closest in age to Harold, but as boys, these two were the least attached and it was not until later in life that they learned to appreciate each other's qualities.

Wilfred was educated at the Birkenhead Institute and under his mother's influence developed into an earnest and slightly arrogant young man. In 1907 the Owens moved again - this time to Shrewsbury as Wilfred's father, Tom, had been appointed Assistant Superintendent of the Joint Railways. Their living conditions improved, especially with the addition of the open countryside which was now close at hand. Wilfred's seat of education became the Technical School in Shrewsbury where he studied hard. He enjoyed literature, having begun to write his own poems at about the age of ten and was then, as always, particularly influenced by the works of Keats.

In 1911 he sat the qualifying exam for London University and passed. However, his parents were unable to afford the fees, so he required a scholarship which was out of the question. He took a position as lay assistant to the Vicar of Dunsden in Oxfordshire, in return for which he would receive tuition. This was not a happy time for Wilfred, who found his religious beliefs tested when he was confronted with the harsh realities of lives of the poor people within the parish. The absence of his mother, who had been the greatest influence on his religious viewpoint, did not help matters. These doubts were fuelled by his growing interest in literature and, feeling that the two subjects were completely at odds, he decided to leave Dunsden in February 1913, returning to Shrewsbury. He then sat for a scholarship at Reading University, but failed and decided to put an end to his ambition of a university education.

The financial position of the family meant that a career as a poet was impossible, so Wilfred decided to travel to France and work there as a teacher of English in the Berlitz School of Languages. This was no greater success than Dunsden and following an illness, he left in July 1914 and took up the position of private tutor to a wealthy family in the Pyrenees. In the autumn, however, he left this job and took up a similar one with another family which lasted until August 1915.

The outbreak of war initially had little effect on Owen, who continued with his life in France. In a letter to his mother from Bordeaux, dated 2nd December 1914, he speaks of his shame at not enlisting, but justifies this with the knowledge that he is perpetuating the English language: an ideal which he seems to have found more important than any other at that time. By July 1915, he showed the first signs of a change of mind. In another letter to his mother, this time dated the 25th July 1915, he comments that his inner happiness is now at stake. He says that he has decided to enlist as he can no longer continue to sit on the side-lines while others are fighting.

Owen returned to England in September 1915 and enlisted in the Artists' Rifles in October. Following months of training, he was commissioned into the Manchester Regiment in June 1916. Second

Lieutenant Wilfred Owen arrived in France in late December 1916, right in the middle of the coldest winter of the war. He was sent to Beaumont Hamel on the Somme as one of 527 reinforcements sent out following heavy losses in the Ancre Offensive.

His letters to his mother from this period reflect his shock at the conditions both in the trenches and behind the lines. He also speaks movingly of his pity for his fellow soldiers and their suffering, especially in the extreme cold of that particular winter, when men were known to freeze to death. His language, even in these simple letters, is evocative, making the reader truly understand the deprivation and hardship brought on by the war.

On 13th March 1917, Owen fell into a cellar and although he initially thought he had just banged his head, he had in fact received a concussion which hospitalised him for two weeks. On his return to his battalion at the beginning of April, he found himself involved in heavy fighting near St Quentin. He was blown off his feet by a shell in Savy Wood and spent several days in a shell-hole surrounded by the dismembered remains of a fellow officer. Although physically unhurt, when Owen's Battalion was relieved on 21st April, it was noticed that his behaviour had become abnormal - he was confused in his speech and appeared shaky. He was diagnosed as suffering from shell-shock and was sent to a Casualty Clearing Station. Eventually he was sent to Craiglockhart War Hospital in Edinburgh, where he would remain for four months.

While at Craiglockhart, Owen met Siegfried Sassoon, a fellow patient, and the two became friends. Sassoon's reputation as a poet and decorated war hero, had preceded him and the shy, stammering Owen was in awe, but plucked up his courage and introduced himself to the older man. After an initially awkward interview, Sassoon agreed to look at some of Owen's work. Whilst these early efforts were by no means brilliant, Sassoon perceived a natural talent hidden in some of Owens' poems. The more experienced poet encouraged and assisted his young protégé, even to the point where the manuscript of one of Owen's most famous poems, *Anthem for Doomed Youth*, contains nine amendments and several crossings-out in Sassoon's handwriting.

It was at this time, and also under the influence of Sassoon, that Owen wrote *Dulce et Decorum Est*, which was a response to the propagandist poems of Jessie Pope and those like her, who goaded young men into joining up, when they had little or no comprehension of what was involved. Sassoon also took the opportunity to introduce Owen to Robert Graves, and through him Owen also met Robert Ross and H. G. Wells, among many others. This introduction into literary circles improved Owen's chances of getting his work published, in which he was encouraged by Sassoon and his friends.

There remains a mystery as to the exact nature of Owen's strong feelings for Sassoon and to what extent these were returned. Whether Owen's emotions stemmed from a romantic love, or hero worship, is not clear but that he harboured a strong attachment for his older friend is well documented in his surviving letters.

Owen was declared fit for light duties and left Craiglockhart in October 1917, bound for Scarborough. By the end of August 1918, he was back in France, having been passed fit for General Service Overseas. Before leaving England he had told his brother, Harold, of his desire to return to the front, despite his, almost certain, knowledge that he would be killed. He had also, encouraged by Robert Ross and Osbert Sitwell, started planning a volume of poetry for publication.

In October 1918, he was awarded the Military Cross. The citation read:

"He personally manipulated a captured machine gun in an isolated position and inflicted considerable losses on the enemy. Throughout he behaved most gallantly."

On the morning of 4th November, while attempting to cross the Sambre-Oise Canal, Owen was shot and killed. One week later, the Armistice was signed, hostilities ceased and all over England, church bells rang out in celebration. Tom and Susan Owen were listening to these bells and looking forward to the safe return of their beloved eldest son when, by a terrible twist of fate, the telegram arrived announcing his death.

Wilfred Owen is buried in the tiny Commonwealth War Graves Commission cemetery at Ors.

Very few of Owen's poems were published during his lifetime and initially his work was not critically acclaimed. The first edition of his poems appeared in 1920, edited by Siegfried Sassoon and Edith Sitwell. It contained less than 25 of his poems. This was followed in 1931 by another volume, this time edited by Edmund Blunden, with a short memoir and extracts from Owen's letters, which gave readers an insight into Owen's life and the thoughts behind his poetry.

It may have taken more than fifty years for Owen to gain the reputation he now holds, but he has become the most widely read and studied war poet.

ROBERT GRAVES

Robert Graves does not appear in the play, but his name is mentioned during the course of conversations between Sassoon and Owen. He played an important part in their lives and this short biography should provide students of this play with sufficient information to understand his character and influence.

Robert Von Ranke Graves was born in Wimbledon on 24th July 1895 to Alfred Perceval Graves and his second wife, Amalie. He was educated at Charterhouse School and had just won a scholarship to St John's College, Oxford, when the First World War began. Graves enlisted in the Royal Welch Fusiliers and was sent to the Western Front. Although not generally a popular officer, Graves formed one particular friendship: with Siegfried Sassoon. The two men discussed poetry and discovered a mutual friend in Edward Marsh.

On 20th July, during the Battle of the Somme, Graves was caught in shellfire and received serious wounds to his thigh and chest. The battalion doctor, Captain J. C. Dunn, believed that these injuries were too severe for Graves to survive and in the belief that nothing could be done for him, he was simply left on a stretcher. The following morning, it was discovered that he was still alive and he was immediately transferred to the field hospital at Heilly. In the meantime, however, the casualty list had been prepared and a letter of condolence sent to his parents.

In fact, although Graves was making slow progress, he had by now arrived at Rouen, from where he sent a scribbled note to his parents. This led to several days of confusion at Graves's family home in Wimbledon. It was not until 30th July that his parents received official confirmation that their son was still alive and would shortly arrive in England, which he duly did on 3rd August. By this time, the Times newspaper had printed his name among the casualty lists - which they subsequently retracted on August 5th.

Graves recovered fairly quickly and, by the end of August, he was at his parent's holiday home in Harlech, where he was joined by Siegfried Sassoon, who was also convalescing. The two men then travelled to Kent to visit Sassoon's mother. Graves had, however, suffered serious damage to his lungs - although he managed to pass a medical board on November 17th, returning to France in January 1917. His damaged lungs proved worse than expected and he succumbed to a bout of pneumonia. While recovering in England, it also became clear that he was suffering from shell-shock. Following a fall down some stairs, he was sent to Osborne House on the Isle of Wight to recuperate.

In July 1917, Sassoon made a public Declaration against the war and upon hearing of this, Graves was horrified. He felt that action was needed to make Sassoon see sense, so he got the medical board to declare him fit for home service and travelled to London where he met Edward Marsh and Robbie Ross before travelling to the regimental headquarters at Litherland. Here he found Sassoon, holding out for a court-martial, so Graves swore on an imaginary Bible that the authorities would never allow Sassoon to be disciplined in this way, but planned to have him declared insane and incarcerated. This gamble paid off and Sassoon agreed to appear before a medical board which announced that Sassoon was suffering from neurosis and sent him to Craiglockhart Hospital in Edinburgh for 'treatment'.

In January 1918, Robert married Nancy Nicholson, the daughter of old family friends and once he was demobilised, his thoughts turned towards an occupation. Nancy gave birth to their first child, Jenny, on 6th January 1919, so the need to earn a living was becoming more pressing than before. However, by that autumn, Robert had decided to resume his education (which came with a grant of £200.00 per annum). By the time Robert took up his place at Oxford, in October, Nancy was pregnant again and their second child, David, was born on 7th March 1920. Money continued to be a problem, especially when Robert's shell-shock resurfaced. He decided to postpone his degree and he and Nancy moved to a house named The World's End at Islip in Oxfordshire which was owned by Robert's mother. Their second daughter, Catherine, was born on 3rd February 1922, followed by Sam on January 4th 1924. Financial difficulties continued and Graves borrowed from his parents and friends, including Sassoon.

Having finally gained his degree in 1925, Graves reluctantly accepted the role of English Professor at Cairo University, which brought with it a substantial salary. In January 1926, therefore, the whole family left England, accompanied by the American poet Laura Riding, with whom Robert hoped to collaborate on several projects. Life in Cairo proved disappointing and within six months, they had returned to Oxfordshire.

Laura Riding came to have a huge influence over Robert and eventually they became lovers. Nancy initially left Robert, but returned and a peculiar ménage was set up. Laura, who believed herself to be a Goddess, needed to control the people (but particularly men) around her. When this failed she was prone to extreme actions, which once included throwing herself from a fourth floor window.

By September 1929, Robert's autobiography, *Goodbye to all That*, was finished and he and Laura moved to Majorca. In their wake they left bitter recriminations about both their lifestyle and the content of his book. Edward Marsh insisted that Robert had misrepresented him and forced the publishers to insert an erratum slip into every copy to that effect. In addition, Siegfried Sassoon was livid at Robert's inclusion of one of his poems and, more importantly, his description of their visit to his family home in 1916 which he felt would be bound to cause offence to his mother. To avoid a lawsuit, the publishers replaced the necessary passages with asterisks.

Laura and Robert began to build their own house in the village of Deyá, and Laura continued to 'play' with the emotions of others, surrounding herself with disciples, giving no regard to the relationships of others or to their own happiness. Robert, meanwhile, had begun working on his historical novel, entitled *I, Claudius*, which was completed in 1933 and sold well.

In 1936 Robert and Laura were forced to leave Majorca due to the Spanish Civil War and fled, initially to England and then to northern France, where they were joined by their old friend Alan Hodge and his new wife, Beryl. In 1939, Robert and Laura decided to go to America, where Laura was keen to meet the critic Schuyler Jackson and again they were joined by Alan and Beryl Hodge. Laura immediately set her sights on Jackson, but first needed to eliminate his wife, Kit. Laura systematically wore her down until, within six weeks, she was declared insane and placed in an asylum. Having denied Robert a physical relationship for over 10 years, Laura almost immediately became Jackson's lover. Those who had witnessed these events, believed themselves to have been in the presence of someone truly evil. Robert fled America and returned to England, followed by Beryl, who had grown very attached to him.

Alan Hodge agreed to divorce Beryl and remained on excellent terms with her and Robert for the rest of his life. Nancy, on the other hand, refused Robert's request for a divorce so Robert and Beryl moved in together. Before long Beryl was pregnant with her first child, William, who was born in September 1940. During this same month, David, Robert's oldest son, followed in his father's footsteps and enlisted in the Royal Welch Fusiliers. Jenny and Catherine also enlisted in the WAAF's, but Sam's deafness would prevent him from serving in the armed forces in the Second World War. In April 1943, David was shot and believed killed while serving in Burma, although his family did not received final confirmation of this until after the war.

Later that year, Beryl gave birth to her second child, a daughter named Lucia, followed in December 1944 by another son, Juan. Once the war was over, Robert, Beryl and the children moved back to Dejá. Late in 1949, Nancy finally divorced Robert and he and Beryl were married on May 11th 1950.

Domestic bliss did not sit well with Robert's poetic requirements and he craved another muse. His first inspiration came in the form of Judith Bledsoe, a 17-year-old American beauty who Beryl accepted, realising that Robert needed someone to inspire his greatest poetry - as she herself had done at the beginning of their relationship. Judith found Robert's possessive nature intolerable and before long, she left. In January 1953, Beryl gave birth to her final child - Tomas.

Robert began to undertake lecture tours of America which proved very lucrative and the next few years were more calm. In June 1960, Robert came across his next muse: Margot Callas, with whom he immediately fell in love. Beryl remained unperturbed by this and Margot moved into a nearby cottage. The following year, Margot fell in love herself: with a friend of Roberts - Alastair Reid. Robert was distraught and blamed Reid entirely.

In 1961, Robert was elected as Professor of Poetry at Oxford University. Two years later he began a relationship with Cindy Lee, who came the closest of all his muses to dividing him and Beryl. During their relationship, Cindy changed her name first to Emile Laraçuen, then to Aemile and then Aemilia. She brought Robert great joy, but also great pain as her behaviour was frequently wild. Robert contemplated leaving Beryl on more than one occasion, but always returned.

Tragedy struck in February 1964 when Robert and Nancy's oldest child, Jenny, died suddenly at the age of just 45. Robert did not attend her funeral. His passion for Aemilia continued until 1966 when she was replaced by Julia Simon (know as Juli to Robert). This platonic relationship continued until Robert's death.

By the early 1970s Graves was showing signs of memory loss and his eyesight was beginning to fail. He relied heavily on Beryl. 1975 brought Robert's 80th birthday and the following year saw the screening of the BBC production of *I, Claudius* the royalties from which ensured financial security.

As Robert's memory worsened, the task of looking after him became more of a strain and Beryl enlisted the help of his daughter, Catherine and eventually nurses were brought in to assist further. Nancy Nicholson died in 1977, following a long illness and then in 1979, Alan Hodge passed away.

Under Beryl's loyal and unstinting care, Robert lived to see his 90th birthday on 24th July 1985. His health continued to deteriorate and on December 7th, he died peacefully, with Beryl, as ever, holding his hand.

ROBBIE ROSS

Although not a character in this play, Robbie Ross played an integral part in the lives of both Sassoon and Owen. As such, the following biographical detail provides the reader with some background information on this influential, but often overlooked, character.

Robert Baldwin Ross (known as Bobby or Robbie) was born on 25th May 1869 in the town of Tours in France. He was the youngest of the five surviving children of John Ross and his wife Augusta (known as Eliza). John Ross had trained and practiced as a lawyer in Canada before being appointed Attorney General. Three years before Robert was born, the family moved from Canada to Tours, despite the fact that John Ross had just been appointed as a member of the newly founded Canadian Senate. In the year of Robert's birth, his father was chosen to become the Senate Speaker, which meant the family had no choice but to go back to Canada. The timing of this appointment seemed fortuitous as it meant the family avoided the upheaval of the Franco-Prussian war which began in July 1870.

The return to Canada was, however, disastrous for the family. Upon his arrival, John Ross discovered that his business associate had been embezzling their clients' money. The strain of this, his moral obligation to repay the misappropriated funds and the responsibility of his new position led to his untimely death in January 1871. Just three months later, Eliza returned to Europe, but as France was still in turmoil, she chose to settle in London.

Young Robert was a delicate boy and Eliza was mindful of this, charging his older brothers, John and Alexander with the task of looking after him if she were absent. Initially Robert was educated at Sandroyd Preparatory School at Cobham in Surrey before winning a scholarship to Clifton College near Bristol at the age of thirteen. His mother, however, decided that Robert was too weak to cope with school and he continued his education at home. He travelled with his mother on her frequent trips to Europe and learnt to appreciate art. His brother Alexander also introduced Robert to his literary friends, but no matter how good his connections, nothing could make up for a lack of formal education. It was decided that Robert should attend a 'crammers' school in Covent Garden, where within two years he would be able to gain the necessary qualifications to apply for a place at University.

While his mother was travelling abroad, she wanted him to lodge with a respectable family and for this purpose, she chose Mr and Mrs Oscar Wilde. Ross spent several months in 1887 at 16 Tite Street, Chelsea - home of the rising dramatist and his family. Unbeknownst to anyone else, Ross and Wilde were already acquainted. Initially, theirs was an intimate relationship, but it soon developed into a deep and lasting friendship, with Ross becoming Wilde's most loyal and protective ally, particularly during his trial, bankruptcy and imprisonment.

Once Wilde was released from prison, he lived on the Continent and his health deteriorated. Ross was with Wilde when he died on 30th November 1900 in Paris. As Wilde's literary executor Ross ensured that the copyright of Wilde's work was returned to his sons and that Wilde's bankruptcy was cleared. His fierce loyalty to Wilde made him a dangerous enemy in the form of Lord Alfred Douglas, Wilde's former lover who would hound Ross for the rest of his life.

From 1901 to 1909 Ross and his friend More Adey ran the Carfax Gallery. Then Ross became an art critic on the *Morning Post* before taking a position as the art valuer for the Inland Revenue.

On 17th October 1915, Ross was introduced to Siegfried Sassoon and a friendship was immediately formed between them. Sassoon admired Ross's sense of humour and defiance of authority but, most especially, his loyalty - a trait which Sassoon valued probably more than any other. During his leave in early 1916, Sassoon stayed at 40 Half Moon Street - Ross's address - and eventually took rooms there himself. Ross helped Sassoon come to terms with his confusion over his sexuality and the poet entrusted Ross with the manuscripts of his work, going on to dedicate his second volume, *Counter-Attack*, to Ross. In the summer of 1916, Lord Alfred Douglas began his latest campaign against Ross, leading Sassoon and other friends to worry about his health.

During 1917, as Sassoon planned his *Declaration*, he intentionally remained aloof from Ross, anxious to avoid involving his friend in any further scandal. However, once the *Declaration* had been sent to his Commanding Officer, Sassoon sent Ross, among others, a copy. Despite his own anti-war feelings, Ross was horrified and immediately wrote to Sassoon, expressing his genuine fear as to the consequences of his actions. Ross then contacted Robert Graves and the two men discussed the best possible course of action, with Ross also making use of his War Office contacts. The actions of Sassoon's friends culminated in a Medical Board, rather than a court-martial.

Later in 1917, Sassoon sent another letter to Ross: this time introducing his friend to its bearer - Wilfred Owen. Ross took the young poet under his wing and introduced him to the London literary circle.

In July 1918, released from Craiglockhart and back in France, Sassoon was shot in the head. He survived this and found himself in hospital in London, where one of the few people permitted to visit him was Ross. Once out of hospital, the two men continued to meet regularly. On 4th October 1918, Sassoon, despite feeling unwell, paid a visit to Ross at Half Moon Street. Ross was due to leave for Australia to act as a consultant to the Melbourne Art

Gallery and Sassoon was keen to see him before his departure. Ross also appeared unwell that evening and when they were unexpectedly joined by the writer Charles Scott Moncrieff and a young actor, Noel Coward, Sassoon decided to take his leave. Ross followed him downstairs to say a private farewell, before returning to his remaining guests. The following day, Robbie Ross died of heart failure, aged 49. The gap which he left in the lives of those he knew was too great even for them to fully appreciate.

In accordance with his wishes, Ross's ashes were placed in Oscar Wilde's tomb in Paris.

EDWARD MARSH

Friend, confidant, mentor and supporter of many young artists, writers and poets in the early twentieth century, Edward Marsh was born in London on 18th November 1872. His father, Frederick was a prominent surgeon and his mother, Jane, was the founder of the Alexander Hospital for Children with Hip Disease. Marsh was educated at Westminster School and then at Trinity College, Cambridge where he studied Classics and gained a great appreciation for art and literature.

Through his dealings in the art world, he came to know Robbie Ross and through the author and critic Edmund Gosse, he was also introduced to many in the London literary circle. In 1912 Marsh, together with Rupert Brooke and Wilfrid Wilson Gibson, was one of the founders of the anthologies of *Georgian Poetry*, of which he also became the editor. Later editions of these anthologies would include work by Siegfried Sassoon, Robert Graves and Robert Nichols, to name but a few. Marsh insisted on dealing with the royalty payments himself, which placed him in a good position for helping the young poets when they found themselves in financial difficulties. Marsh also became a close friend of Ivor Novello, who used his rooms at Raymond Building, Grays Inn for composing his many popular songs.

As well as his interests in art and literature, Marsh also worked as a Civil Servant and in 1906 he became Private Secretary to Winston Churchill. His position in the government helped him to plead for leniency on behalf of his friend Siegfried Sassoon, following publication of Sassoon's anti-war Declaration in 1917.

Following his retirement, in 1937, Marsh was knighted. He retained an interest in the arts, becoming a Trustee of the Tate Gallery. Edward Marsh died in London on 13th January 1953.

H. G. WELLS

Herbert George Wells was born on 21st September 1866, the youngest of the five children of Joseph and Sarah Wells. Although the family owned a china shop, the income from this was insufficient and Herbert's parents were forced to put their sons forward for apprenticeships, following their educations. Sarah also, effectively, left her family and returned to domestic service. Herbert tried several professions, including chemist's assistant and draper's apprentice and his experiences in this latter position provided the inspiration for his later novel, *Kipps*.

Nothing that he tried was suitable and Herbert much preferred the employment of reading to any other. Eventually, however, he settled as a teacher/pupil at a Sussex grammar school, enabling him to continue with his education and earn a living. In 1887 Wells became a full-time teacher and continued in this profession until writing became his main occupation in 1893.

Meanwhile, In 1891, Wells married his cousin Isabel. This was a short marriage, however, as Wells left his wife in 1894 and married Amy Catherine Robbins with whom he had two sons, George and Frank. While he was married, Wells had several extra-marital affairs and two other children, including a son, Anthony with the novelist Rebecca West. Amy was aware of his infidelity, but they remained married until her death in 1927.

Wells' novels include *The Time Machine*, *The Invisible Man* and *The War of the Worlds*, although during his lifetime, he was as well known for his political thinking as for his writing. He became a member of the Fabian Society but left when the other members declined his suggestion to turn the Society into a more radical pressure group. H. G. Wells died on August 13th 1946.

ARNOLD BENNETT

Arnold Bennett was born on 27th May 1867 in Staffordshire. He was educated in Newcastle-under-Lyme and in 1888 he moved to London and found work as a clerk in a solicitor's office. The following year, he entered and won and literary competition in a magazine. This triumph persuaded him to pursue a career in journalism. While working as assistant editor of the magazine *Woman*, he also began writing stories and in 1898, he first novel was published. In 1900, he gave up editing and became a full time writer.

In 1902, following the death of his father, Bennett moved to Paris where he married Marie Marguerite Soulie five years later. The couple initially lived in France but in 1912 they moved to Thorpe-le-Soken in Essex.

When the First World War began, the War Propaganda Bureau asked Bennett and twenty-four other prominent authors, including G K Chesterton, Thomas Hardy, H G Wells and Rudyard Kipling, to write in support of Britain's war effort. During the war over one thousand pamphlets were produced, although the existence of the War Propaganda Bureau remained a secret until 1935. In 1918, Bennett was also asked to sit on the British War Memorial Committee, whose task was to choose artists to produce official war paintings. The artists selected included Stanley Spencer, John Nash and John Singer Sargent.

Following the end of the First World War, Bennett turned his attention back to writing. His marriage ended in 1921 when he and his wife separated and Bennett became involved with the actress Dorothy Cheston. They lived together, and had one daughter, named Virginia, although they never married. Arnold Bennett died from typhoid fever on March 27th 1931.

THEMES

MALE RELATIONSHIPS

Given the subject matter of this play, it is hardly surprising that the relationships forged during the war between men should be its central theme. The nature of the friendship between Sassoon and Owen develops through the play and Stephen MacDonald shows us Owen's initial deference and admiration blossoming in conjunction with his poetry. Sassoon, on the other hand, is portrayed as someone who gradually mellows towards the younger man, overcoming his natural cynicism and diffidence to develop a respect for Owen's work, along with a deep and abiding personal affection.

While both characters are portrayed as troubled by their experiences, it is Owen who shows the most obvious physical symptoms of neurosis. Sassoon is, therefore, portrayed as something of a saviour: discovering Owen's hidden talents and drawing them out. By the time Owen leaves Craiglockhart, he is seen as a much more confident and self assured person - traits which he owes to his friendship with Sassoon and the acknowledgement of his abilities as a poet.

Their entire relationship, as portrayed in this play, focuses on poetry and the war and how one can influence the other. Their poetry reflects their feelings about the conflict. Their discussion of the conditions at Passchendaele in Act One, for example, shows that they can never escape from the war. Sassoon's growing feelings and concern for Owen are also demonstrated in this scene, as he worries that his young friend might soon be called upon to return to the front.

There is also an underlying reticence and awkwardness in Sassoon's reactions to Owen, who is much more open. This is a reflection of their very different backgrounds. Owen, we are told, has a frank and close relationship with his mother, while Sassoon is much more withdrawn and reluctant to reveal his true feelings to anyone. Owen's initial shyness with Sassoon stems from his awe of the older man and his reputation as a decorated officer and published poet. Owen is also doubtful about his own conduct and Sassoon's references to his colonel embarrass Owen.

There is a strength of feeling displayed between the two men during their time together, although it would appear that Owen harbours the more powerful emotions. Sassoon, evidently, only discovers his true feelings for Owen once they have parted, and especially, with the benefit of hindsight, after Owen's death. His solitary scenes, where he looks back on their time together, show the impact of Owen's death on his character and his delay in appreciating his young friend's qualities, both as a poet and a man.

The friendship between Owen and Sassoon was of only a few months duration, as both men were eventually called upon to return to their duties and Owen, ultimately, to his death. During the play, most of what we learn about them is from Sassoon's perspective, as he reminisces about their time at Craiglockhart. Owen's feelings are portrayed in his letters and appear to be more emotional, although this may only be because Owen was better at expressing himself at the time.

There is no suggestion of a physical relationship between the two men within the play. In fact, their embrace, while highly charged and tender, seems also to cause them some embarrassment. This applies more particularly to Sassoon and may demonstrate his natural diffidence, but could also show that he has an understandable fear of public demonstrations of affection between two men.

As such, this portrayal of their friendship, shows that men were capable of forming deep emotional bonds without the need for any form of physical contact. They could, and frequently did, form lasting attachments, which were emotionally comparable to marriage, but if anything the bonds between these men were stronger - made so by their shared experiences of horror and hardship.

FEELINGS ABOUT THE WAR

Sassoon's feelings about the war are made quite clear early in the play, as he recites his *Declaration*. Owen's experiences at the front have left him mentally scarred and he is clearly angry and bitter, although initially at least, he is less well able to express this either in speech or in his poetry. This helps to demonstrate the effects which the war had on different individuals: Sassoon angrily rebelled; Owen, no less angry, became insular and isolated.

Within the play, both men realise that the war has become their reason for writing and both of them feel a responsibility to report the truth about conditions and the fighting to those at home. Despite his past experiences and his fear, Owen feels that he must return to the fighting to prove to himself that he is not afraid: that he is worthy. Sassoon's reaction to this is to show compassion and understanding. He reveals as much as he can of his own experiences, despite the need to really suppress these memories, but even this is not enough to assuage Owen's guilt, or his need to find out about himself.

Once Sassoon has been shot and Owen visits him in the hospital, Sassoon's actions and feelings become clearer as he explains the full circumstances surrounding the death of David Thomas and the effect this had on him. This scene demonstrates with great clarity, Sassoon's attitude. His anger is shown, but so is his deep emotional tie to those for whom he cares, together with his regrets for the loss of his friend David. Owen, quite rightly, refuses to accept Sassoon's descriptions of himself and his actions, pointing out that all he has really been talking about is love.

Sassoon's desire to return to the front stems, not from a need to prove himself - he has already done that and knows that it achieves nothing - but comes entirely from feelings of guilt. He already knows what his own reactions will be and understands that his death may follow, but he cannot remain safe at Craiglockhart while the men he loves are continuing to fight.

Owen and Sassoon are both angry at what they perceive to be the pointless waste of lives, but this does not prevent them from doing their duty. Instead, they channel their anger into their poetry. In fact, Sassoon wrote some of his best pieces while at Craiglockhart and his influence can be seen in many of the poems which Owen composed after that time. Without their feelings of anger and resentment, as well as their ability to care for others, it is doubtful that either man would have become such a great poet.

COMPARISON

FACT IN FICTION - A CRITICAL ASSESSMENT

The use of well-known and well-reported facts in a work of fiction is always going to be fraught with problems. However, given the subject matter of the First World War, the use of historical facts within fictional works is inevitable. Sometimes problems arise when either that factual element is taken too seriously or too literally, or when the facts themselves are misrepresented or exaggerated. Apart from Stephen MacDonald, among the great number of modern authors who have included realistic elements of the war, or that period, within their novels are Pat Barker (*Regeneration*), Sebastian Faulks (*Birdsong*) and Sebastian Barry (*A Long Long Way*).

When, like Stephen MacDonald, an author's source of information is the letters and memoirs of the deceased, there is a vast responsibility on him not to misrepresent or misinterpret their words, simply because they are no longer able to correct him. In his introduction to this play, Stephen MacDonald makes it clear that the words involved are his: he has 'borrowed' from Sassoon and Owen, but used his own words to tell their story. However, for the reader or audience, this can be easily forgotten, especially with the inclusion of their poetry, which adds to the authenticity and, one can begin to believe that the two men actually said and did *everything* that is represented here. This is, in fact, a tribute to the playwright, who has captured the essence of these men with, sometimes startling, accuracy.

Stephen MacDonald, writing in the early 1980s, without access to Sassoon's diaries, which were yet to be published, represents him as a diffident, yet somewhat tempestuous character. These traits are echoed by Sassoon's most recent biographers, Jean Moorcroft

Wilson, John Stuart-Roberts and Max Egremont, who paint a similar portrait of their subject. Max Egremont, in particular, was granted unprecedented access to Sassoon's papers, giving his portrayal a great depth and clarity and many of the scenes and conversations in the play are confirmed within this biography. That said, the reader or audience must always allow for artistic license: an omission or addition which is necessary to make the play flow better, or condense it down to fit into a reasonable timescale.

This play's subject matter is one of the most famous and influential literary friendships of the First World War - and many might argue, of the twentieth century. Who can say whether Owen's poetry would ever have been published or read had he not summoned up the courage to knock at Sassoon's door in August 1917? The result of this meeting is a matter of historical and literary fact: Wilfred Owen went on to become one of the most widely read and studied poets of the twentieth century, so the impact on Owen could be said to be enormous, although he did not live to see it come to fruition. However, many biographers now agree that this friendship was of much less importance to Sassoon than is implied within this play. Stephen MacDonald points out in his introduction that Sassoon himself did not write about his feelings for Owen until the publication of *Siegfried's Journey* in 1945. In fact, Owen's presence in his life is omitted completely from the earlier Sherston trilogy, although it must also be remembered that Sassoon neglected to point out in these books that he was a poet himself. Given that context, to have written about meeting and influencing Wilfred Owen would have been a little strange.

One fact beyond any doubt, which is admirably reflected in this play, is the depth of emotional attachment which Owen felt for Sassoon. It is clear from his letters, both to his mother and Sassoon himself, that Owen held his new friend in the highest esteem. This was not simply gratitude for Sassoon's assistance in advancing his poetry, but also because he had a genuine affection for the man. In addition Stephen MacDonald manages to realistically convey their necessary restraint in public, as well as their intimate knowledge of each other - faults included - without becoming overly sentimental.

The use of diaries and letters captures a moment in time and it really was just a moment: theirs was the briefest of friendships and yet has spawned much debate ever since. Stephen MacDonald is not alone in sensing the public's interest in this friendship, especially over the precise nature of their relationship, but due to Owen's death and Sassoon's restraint in discussing emotional matters, this question remains unanswered. Some biographers have suggested a physical element, although this seems to be based entirely on the effusive language in Owen's later letters. Erring on the side of caution, MacDonald has chosen to hint at their love, but leaves the audience to decide the full extent of their friendship.

Another author who has chosen to portray the relationship between Owen and Sassoon in a work of fiction, is Pat Barker in *Regeneration*. This, together with the inclusion of other genuine historical elements, such as the Pemberton Billing scandal, gives the novel a necessary air of authenticity. Pat Barker has included notes on her sources and pointed out the factual elements in her novel, which helps the reader to understand the difference between these two facets - the realistic and the fictional.

In the case of *Regeneration*, the main subject is not actually the friendship between Sassoon and Owen - although that is often the part which people remember the most. Instead, this novel is about re-building men whose lives have been shattered by their wartime experiences; it is about human relationships of all kinds, both romantic and otherwise; and it is about the physchological and physical effects of the war on both the soldiers involved and those who must treat them.

These two authors represent Sassoon and Owen's friendship in a similar light - undoubtedly due to the limited resources which are available. These representations encapsulate, for many, their understanding not only of the 'war poet' in general, but also of the time through which they were living. The First World War shaped these men - and many others - and those who survived knew that they had been changed beyond recognition. Stephen MacDonald, by giving Sassoon the benefit of 14 years' hindsight, is able to demonstrate the long term effects of the war, the loss of a loved-one and the sense of having to force oneself to overcome the depression, guilt and hopelessness which can accompany such an experience. Thus this play is given an uplifting end - reflecting Sassoon's genuine understanding that, although he and others had lost a great many friends, they now had a responsibility to carry on.

While historical novels and plays, by their very nature have a duty to be as accurate as possible, the authors must also maintain a realistic element in their characters and plot. If the reader or audience cannot believe in the story-line or empathise with the characters, no amount of factual accuracy will suffice. Both Stephen MacDonald and Pat Barker, by using genuine people in their works have taken advantage of the fact that many of their readers will already be aware of Owen and Sassoon, possibly know something about their lives and want to learn more - thus capturing their interest right from the start. This is not always the case in a piece which involves entirely fictitious characters and it could be argued that if the reader loses interest in the outcome of the story, it might be because they simply can't bring themselves to care about the people involved.

That is not to say that the reader has to like the characters: Billy Prior in *Regeneration* is not a pleasant man. He is coarse, opinionated and cynical, and yet the reader wants to find out what has happened to him; why he is at Craiglockhart and what occurred to make him mute. In addition, the tiny glimpses of a different side to Billy, which the reader gets, show that most of his reactions are bravado - that there is more to Billy than meets the eye. As such, even once his past torment is revealed, the reader still maintains an interest in his future. This could not necessarily be said of the two other novels mentioned earlier: the central characters in both *Birdsong* and *A Long Long Way* fail to inspire the reader and one can, therefore, quickly lose interest in their experiences.

Sebastian Barry's novel *A Long Long Way* tells the story of Willie Dunne, a young Irishman, who decides to fight for the Allies against the Germans. The backdrop for Dunne's war is the Easter Uprising in Ireland and the political and military unrest in his native country, which haunt him despite his own harrowing experiences in the trenches.

Willie Dunne is unfortunately a stereotype who experiences almost every appalling atrocity one can think of. He is gassed, shot at, blown up; his friends die around him, one of them executed; he has the imprint of a comrade's medal burned onto his chest in an explosion; he loses his girlfriend after another friend writes to tell her that he slept with a prostitute; he is shell-shocked and then 'miraculously' cured following a maternal embrace from a nurse. Despite all of this, although Willie becomes angry and confused about the war and the problems in Ireland, his character remains, essentially, the same from beginning to end. As such, some readers may find Willie implausible - at which point, because one can no longer believe in him, one ceases to care about what happens to him.

This book, which was nominated for the Man Booker Prize in 2005, has been widely praised for both its style and historical accuracy. How well deserved this latter praise is, however, remains a matter of debate. Such a glaring error as Barry's assertion (in Chapter

Fourteen) that the [front] line stretched between *Portugal* and the sea, cannot be overlooked and has the regrettable and distracting effect of making any reader, with an interest in history, spend their time searching for further misdemeanours, rather than reading the novel for itself.

Similarly, *Birdsong* by Sebastian Faulks, could be said to suffer from the inclusion of a disproportionate number of details, events and stereotypical opinions, all converging on one man - Stephen Wraysford. These include Wraysford being left for dead and then discovered to be still alive - an episode which is reminiscent of events which occurred in the life of the poet Robert Graves; then he is rescued from the collapsed tunnel by a German doctor, who turns out to be the brother of another soldier for whose death Wraysford had been responsible - thus enabling these two men to demonstrate the element of forgiveness within the conflict. In addition, there is the situation of Wraysford, being stranded in no man's land at the beginning of the Battle of the Somme and then rescued by his best friend, Weir, who despite the confusion, has managed to find exactly the right shell-hole. These events may have their origins in reality, but if so, it seems a little contrived for them to all happen to the same character. It would also be useful for the reader to know from where Sebastian Faulks obtained his information, otherwise the war-time sections of the novel risk becoming a series of implausible events joined together by graphic battle scenes.

Once again, the central character fails to evoke the sympathy of the reader. He has had a harsh childhood; has a torrid yet doomed love affair; he experiences extreme horrors and appalling hardships during the war which result in him becoming mute following the end of the conflict. Despite all of this, it is hard to feel anything for Wraysford, perhaps because everything that happens to him seems a little too artificial.

In addition, some of these modern novels suffer from the author's desire to include scenes of an explicit sexual nature. Given the adage that 'sex sells', this is hardly surprising, but whether these scenes actually add, or are necessary, to the plot is debatable.

The authors named above all have one thing in common: namely that they have no first-hand experience of the war and their works are based entirely on research. Others, who have written with the benefit of a personal knowledge of the conflict tend to portray a more intimate snapshot. In the case of *Journey's End* by R.C. Sherriff the action takes place over just three days, and is entirely confined to a British dugout. This enables the reader or audience to become better acquainted with the characters, because one is not always trying to keep up with the countless catastrophic events surrounding them. *All Quiet on the Western Front* by Erich Maria Remarque spans most of the war and yet his characters are still rounded and realistic, possibly because they are based on his real experiences and the friendships he formed while serving during the war. Both Sherriff and Remarque ably demonstrate the point that much of a soldier's time was spent waiting for something to happen and they capture both the tension and boredom of this situation.

With such a widely researched subject matter, novels and plays on the First World War, whenever they are written should engage the reader, making them want to know more and retaining their interest in the characters from beginning to end. In addition, the really good ones - rather than those which just achieve commercial success - will also have the ability to make their readers or audiences want to know more - thus inspiring the next generation and doing justice to a 'lost' one.

OH WHAT A LOVELY WAR
BY JOAN LITTLEWOOD'S THEATRE WORKSHOP

INTRODUCTION

This play, which was first performed on stage in 1963, is - at least according to the source list - based on a wide collection of First World War material, ranging from the memoirs of poets such as Robert Graves, Siegfried Sassoon and Edmund Blunden to the official histories and diaries of the time. As such, one might imagine that it would provide a definitive view of the war and yet, this is precisely what it stands accused of failing to provide.

The production company chose to satirise the war; to ridicule the leaders of the day; and to treat the subject and the performance in an unorthodox manner. As such, what they created is unique. The play, which reflected the feelings of many at the time, with regard to the loss of life and futile nature of the conflict, can now appear outdated and inaccurate, especially in light many of the more recent and positive assertions as to the conduct of the war.

Despite all of this, *Oh What a Lovely War* remains an interesting subject for study. Due to the individual nature of this play, the format of this study guide is, necessarily, different from most of our other titles. Rather than a more conventional examination of themes and comparisons, we have provided a more critical perspective, which is based upon my opinion of the play and its interpretation by critics and historians.

SYNOPSIS

ACT ONE

Summer 1914. The Master of Ceremonies (MC) introduces 'the show', which takes the form of a war game. Representatives of the various major European powers debate their stances in the event of war. Then the Germans, represented by the Kaiser and General von Moltke, discuss the Schlieffen Plan. The French, Russians and British all discuss their own plans - although the British plan seems non-existent, other than a dependence on the Royal Navy.

The action switches to Sarajevo and the shooting of Archduke Franz Ferdinand and his wife Sophie. Two disguised secret policemen (one a Serbian and the other from Austria-Hungary) humorously talk over the shooting. They then reveal their true identities before arresting a nearby stallholder for no apparent reason. Various characters discuss the mobilisation of Russia and France, the German advance into Belgium and Britain's reaction, creating the impression that Europe is going to war because it has lost control and that nobody really understands what is happening or the consequences of their actions.

Once war has been declared, the MC announces that this concludes the first part of the war game. The scene changes to Belgium, where the Belgians and French attempt to hold back the Germans. They have some initial success, but eventually Belgium capitulates. Back in England, men are learning to drill, charge and bayonet the enemy, while women goad young men into joining up.

Meanwhile, in France, the French commander, Lanrezac and his Belgian counterpart, de Moranneville await the arrival of Sir John French and Sir Henry Wilson. When they meet, there is an obvious language barrier, which leads to much confusion. Lanrezac wants the

British troops to come quickly; Sir John French reminds him that Britain is doing her best. Eventually, Sir John awards a medal to Lanrezac on behalf of the King and everyone departs happily.

Following the retreat from Mons, the first of the wounded begin arriving at Waterloo Station. Transport has been provided for the officers, but the men have to wait until a corporal manages to arrange for some civilian lorry drivers to move them to hospital, during their lunch-break.

The war progresses, and it is now winter in the trenches. Some British soldiers play cards, listening to a distant bombardment. Then, they hear a carol being sung and realise the voice is German and it is coming from the trench opposite. When the German soldier has finished his song, he calls out in English and the opposing sides exchange words and gifts before meeting in No Man's Land for the Christmas Truce. The first act closes with exploding shells and the news that many hope that 1915 will bring peace.

ACT TWO

The news, at the opening of this Act, is no improvement - there have been many losses of life and no territorial gains. Women are still goading all able-bodied men to enlist by various means; unscrupulous men from every nation are seen as profiteers, only interested in making money. They are not concerned with peace, knowing that it will result in smaller profits for them.

In the trenches, a group of British soldiers is inspected by their commanding officer - a pompous man with no idea of the conditions in the trenches. The scene switches to London and a dance attended by many senior British officers, including Sir Douglas Haig, who eagerly awaits his promotion to Commander-in-Chief of the British Army, replacing Sir John French, who is also attending the dance. The recent promotion of Sir William Robertson causes some debate, as does the identity of Sir John French's partner.

Once Haig has control of the British Army, he continues with a policy of trench warfare on the Western Front, regardless of the human cost. Raw Irish recruits are thrown into the fray and are slaughtered. Meanwhile, in England, Mrs Pankhurst speaks out publicly against the war, but is heckled by her audience.

On 1st July 1916, the Somme battle commences and despite the mounting casualties, Haig continues to send men over-the-top. He remains undeterred because he knows that Britain has more men than Germany and eventually, if they keep killing each other at the same rate, the law of averages dictates that Britain will win.

A chaplain prays for Haig and for victory; Haig prays for a speedy end to the war, before the Americans arrive to steal his thunder; a nurse prays that the suffering will soon be brought to an end. The news announces that by November 1916 there are more than two million men dead on the Western Front. Haig, meanwhile, thanks

God for success in the battle, although the casualties continue to mount up, and the mud grows deeper all along the front line.

The news continues to worsen, with ever-increasing casualty lists. The girls at home look at the lists and then discuss how much money they are making at the factories. As 1918 opens, all sides still seem to believe that God is with them and victory is in sight, although as to when exactly that will be, there seems to be no answer. By the end of the war, the news announces the vast numbers of dead, injured and missing.

BIOGRAPHIES

Due to the nature of this play, it is not feasible to include an analysis of the characters involved. We have, therefore, provided biographies of two of the main characters involved, together with an appraisal of their role in the war. The following chapter provides an interpretation of their portrayal in this play, thus allowing students to compare their real personalities with their depiction in *Oh What a Lovely War*.

DOUGLAS HAIG

Field Marshal
Sir Douglas Haig
Image courtesy of Photo's of the Great War

Born in Edinburgh on Wednesday 19th June 1861, Douglas Haig was the youngest of eleven children. Haig's father, John, was head of the successful whisky distillery which still bears the family name. Although this background ensured that Haig enjoyed a prosperous upbringing, the social stigma of the family's wealth coming from 'trade' would follow him throughout his life. Douglas Haig was educated at Clifton College in Bristol, before attending Brasenose College, Oxford. Following this he went to the Royal Military College, Sandhurst in 1884, where following a one-year course, he was commissioned into the 7th Hussars.

In 1886, Haig was in India with his regiment and within two years had been promoted to Captain and Adjutant (an administrative officer, acting as assistant to a senior officer). He spent six years in India, during which time he was given command of a squadron, then in 1892 he returned to England to sit the Staff College entrance examination. He failed to pass this and duly returned to India to rejoin the 7th Hussars. Haig remained with his regiment until his appointment as Aide-de-Camp to the Inspector General of Cavalry. This position, which is generally speaking, that of a personal assistant, lasted for one year, at which point Haig became a member of Sir John French's staff, helping to write the new Cavalry Drill Book, the composition of which Haig took over when French left this department.

As a result of his work on this project, the High Command decided in 1896 that Haig should be allowed to enter the Staff College without having to sit the qualifying examination. This decision did not disappoint, as Haig spent a valuable two years there, during which time he greatly impressed his instructors. Following his time at the Staff College in Camberley, Haig left for the Sudan, where he served as a Major during Kitchener's battle with the Dervishes. Returning to England in 1898, he was promoted to Brigade-Major, serving once more under Major-General Sir John French at Aldershot. It was during this time that French borrowed £2,000 from his junior officer, in order to pay his debts. Failure to do this would have resulted in French being forced to resign his commission, so it could be argued that Haig saved his career, although whether he ever repaid the debt to Haig is a matter of conjecture.

The Boer War (1899-1902) found Haig, together with French, in South Africa, where he acquitted himself well and won promotion to the rank of Lieutenant-Colonel. His return to England in 1902 was short-lived and within a year he was back in India as Inspector-General of Cavalry, serving under Lord Kitchener. He remained in this post for three years, during which time he wrote a book - *Cavalry Studies: Strategic and Tactical* in which he erroneously predicted an ever-increasing role for the cavalry in future conflicts.

In 1905, the usually dour and uncommunicative Haig met Dorothy Vivian, and following a one-month courtship, they were married. Dorothy was lady-in-waiting to Queen Alexandra and her position greatly enhanced her husband's social status.

Haig now became Military Secretary to Richard Haldane at the War Office. Here, his work involved assisting with the reorganisation of the British Army, including the formation of the British Expeditionary Force, which it was decided, would be deployed in the event of war. In 1909, Haig was knighted at Balmoral by King Edward VII before sailing with his wife for India, to take up the appoint of Chief of the General Staff to the Commander in Chief.

An offer arrived in 1911 from Haldane. This involved Haig, now a Lieutenant-General, returning to England to take the position of Commanding Officer at Aldershot. On the correct assumption that, in the event of war, the officer holding this position would become commander of the First Corps of the BEF, Haig accepted. Despite his retiring appearance, Haig was extremely ambitious and did not hesitate to use his influence, both in the royal family and in the cabinet, to further his own career.

When war came in August 1914, Haig took the opportunity to use this influence, together with his position as Commander of the First Corps, to criticise the leadership of the Commander-in-Chief, Sir John French. He wrote often of French's unsuitability for the position and during the battles of 1914-1915, their relationship soured further as each would try to blame the other for any failures, particularly during the costly Battle of Loos. Eventually, French could no longer maintain his command and, upon his resignation on 8th December 1915, Haig was appointed Commander-in-Chief of the British Armies in France.

The first real test of Haig's mettle came in the summer of 1916 with the Battle of the Somme. The planning for this began almost as soon as Haig assumed command. The leader of the French forces, Joffre, wanted to launch the attack over a wide front in August of 1916. However, in February, while planning was still in its early stages, the Germans began their assault on Verdun. This changed everything, forcing the French to move their troops further south and leaving the bulk of the fighting on the Somme to the British forces. Haig had not wanted to fight at the Somme in the first place, preferring to concentrate his forces around Ypres, but was under strict instructions to adhere to the wishes of the French forces ahead of his own. The first day of the Battle of the Somme was - and remains - the bloodiest in the history of the British army. Haig is frequently criticised for continuing with the battle, regardless of the loss of life. Indeed, seen from today, his attitude can appear quite callous, as he persisted with the battle for four long months. It is quite difficult, with the benefit of hindsight, to understand why he allowed the slaughter on the Somme and later, at Passchendaele, to carry on, and for this reason, he has become one of the most maligned military leaders in British history.

In recent years, more and more historians are putting the point that there are two sides to this argument. They argue that while Haig almost certainly made mistakes, given the circumstances in which his army was fighting and the political influences involved, he out-performed almost all of his military counterparts. By 1918, with the Russians in the throes of revolution, the French army in tatters and the Americans not yet arrived in sufficient numbers, the British army was effectively fighting alone on the Western Front. Haig had been charged, by the government, with winning the war and he was single-minded enough to do this. Unlike his predecessor, Sir John French, Haig knew and accepted, that lives had to be lost to achieve this aim. His detached attitude does not mean that he enjoyed this process, simply that he knew it had to be done.

During and immediately after the war, Haig was well respected, both by his peers and generally speaking, by those who served under him. In the immediate aftermath of the war, Haig would appear to have retained his popularity among the general public too, but not within government circles. While other generals were rewarded for their war service with large cash gifts and honorary titles, Haig's anticipated Peerage was delayed until 1919. When a cash sum was eventually offered by Parliament, he refused to accept it, until his soldiers had also received their pensions.

Haig went on to use his influence to amalgamate several veteran's associations into the British Legion, which held the first of its annual Poppy Days on the 11th November 1921. Haig continued to be involved in the welfare of his men until his death on 28th January 1928. His funeral was attended by tens of thousands of his former soldiers. In the 1930s the former Prime Minister, David Lloyd George, published his memoirs and this marked the beginning of Haig's downfall and clouded opinion for decades.

JOHN FRENCH

Field Marshal
Sir John French
*Image courtesy of Photo's
of the Great War*

John French was born at Ripple Vale in Kent on 28th September 1852. His father, whose name he shared, was a retired Naval Captain, who died when his son was two years old, leaving his widow to raise their large family, which consisted of John and his six sisters: Mary, Eleanora, Margaret, Caroline, Catherine and Charlotte. Their mother found it difficult to cope and in 1862, when John was ten years old, she was removed from the family home to an institution, where she would die five years later. John's sisters, being much older than him, took over his upbringing.

His sisters were, however, rather preoccupied with their own lives and the running of the family estate, so John was sent to preparatory school at Harrow, where he remained until early 1866, when he left to enroll at Eastman's Naval Academy in Portsmouth. He only stayed there for a short time as he soon passed the entrance examination necessary for him to become a Naval Cadet on HMS Britannia at Dartmouth. Following two and a half years of harsh training, French qualified as a mid-shipman and was assigned to HMS Warrior, based in Lisbon. Although he enjoyed many aspects of Navy life, especially the lifelong friendships he formed, French decided that he would be better suited to a military life on dry land. In November 1870, he resigned from the Navy in order to join the cavalry.

This move angered his sisters, as the cavalry was the most expensive arm of the forces for an officer to enter. However, French worked hard and on 28th February 1874 he was gazetted into the 8th Hussars, although he quickly transferred to the 19th Hussars, garrisoned at Aldershot. French enjoyed his time in Hampshire and began taking a keen interest in the training of the infantry and artillery, as well as his own cavalry brigade. The family home had, by now, been sold and his share of the proceeds gave him a reasonable annual income, on top of his army pay. However, French had never been very good at managing his financial affairs and his debts soon began to mount up. His reputation as a womaniser began at this point, as he took full advantage of his dashing uniform and appealing personality to woo the ladies. Following his regiment's move to Hounslow in Middlesex, French entered into an ill-advised marriage with Isabella Soundy in June 1875. This alliance was kept a secret from his fellow officers, as its general knowledge would have done nothing to further his career and, by 1878, a divorce had been arranged.

In the meantime, in June 1876, the 19th Hussars were posted to Ireland, where French remained for many years, earning promotion to the rank of Captain in 1880, during which year, he also married again. This time, he made a more suitable and advantageous choice: Eleanora Selby-Lowndes, the daughter of a wealthy squire. During their marriage, her fierce loyalty would be severely tested as, following ten years of marital fidelity, he resumed his philandering ways and embarked on a series of indiscreet affairs. Eleanora remained steadfastly loyal to her husband and, despite his affairs, they were genuinely devoted to each other.

Within a year of his marriage, French left Ireland to take the position of adjutant in the Northumberland Hussars and it was here that his first child, John Richard Lowndes was born in 1881. A daughter was born within the year, but died in infancy. A second son, Edward Gerald, was born in December 1883. French now sought to rejoin the 19th Hussars, as they had been posted to active service in Egypt. Initially, the war office refused his request for a transfer, but eventually he succeeded and arrived in Cairo in

October 1884, where he joined the advance to relieve General Gordon at Khartoum, although they arrived too late to save the General's life. French remained in Egypt until 1886, when he returned to England with the rank of Lieutenant-Colonel. Later that year, his daughter Essex Eleanora was born. Two years later, in the spring of 1888, French took command of the 19th Hussars just before the regiment was due to move, once again, to Hounslow. He was only stationed here for a short time, before returning to Aldershot, where his hard work brought him to the attention of the commanding officer.

In September 1891 French left for India with the 19th Hussars, while Eleanora remained in England with their children. He was away for two years, during which time he became embroiled in a regimental scandal when he embarked on an affair with the wife of one of his fellow officers. He was subsequently named in their divorce proceedings and the scandal that followed almost cost him his career. Once back at home, he was placed on the half-pay list, which had a considerable impact on his always strained finances. Whether or not this was done because of the scandal in India is unknown, but the timing is certainly suggestive, especially bearing in mind his previously admired reputation as a commander and horseman.

It would be over a year before French found favour again, when in the autumn of 1894, he was given temporary command of a brigade during cavalry manoeuvres. His good performance here earned him a promotion to full Colonel and a job as Assistant Adjutant-General at Horse Guards, where he wrote the new Cavalry Drill Book. Following this, in the spring of 1897, he went to Canterbury to command the 2nd Cavalry Brigade and remained there for one year before returning, once again, to Aldershot as Major-General, leading the 1st Cavalry Brigade. Although French relished this new responsibility, scandal once again threatened his downfall. This time it was money, rather than women. Large debts, incurred mainly during his period on half-pay, were now becoming embarrassing and may have caused his demise in the cavalry had it not been for the timely interception of Douglas Haig. These two had known each other for approximately four years and Haig, always careful with money, loaned his senior officer £2,000, which saved French's reputation. With this financial misfortune behind him, French was now free to embark on his next overseas adventure and earn the reputation of a great cavalry commander. On 23rd September 1888, French and Haig set sail for South Africa and the Boer War.

French returned in 1902, his reputation greatly enhanced by a sound performance of his duties in South Africa and was duly rewarded with a promotion to the rank of Lieutenant-General and the command of the Aldershot Garrison. During this time, French came into conflict with his superiors, as he continued to insist that the cavalry should be armed with a lance and sword, rather than a rifle. The Boers had used 'mounted infantry' (men who rode to battle, then dismounted and fought on foot) to great effect, but French refused to be swayed and continued to train his cavalry in the traditional manner.

French left Aldershot in 1907 to become Inspector General of the Forces and his rise continued in 1912 when he became Chief of the General Staff. The following year, he was promoted to the rank of Field Marshal. In March 1914, came an event which, had he not already held the rank of Field Marshal, would have ended French's career - 'the Curragh Incident'. Briefly, Home Rule in Ireland, had been passed by Asquith's government and, while popular with Irish Catholics, it was deeply opposed by the Protestants, who, led by Sir Edward Carson, decided to resist the imposition of Home Rule. They armed themselves and threatened rebellion. The British government told the cavalry commander in Dublin - Brigadier-General Hubert Gough - to use live ammunition against armed protestors. An order was issued locally, stating that officers who came from Ulster could go on 'leave' rather than fight their own countrymen and that others, who opposed this action, were at liberty to resign. Almost to a man, the officers of 3 Cavalry Brigade resigned their commissions. This situation needed clarifying quickly. Gough wrote his own clarification statement which he got countersigned by Sir John French and this was forwarded to the British Government who disagreed with these two senior officers. French felt that his position was now untenable and resigned. However, once an officer reaches the rank of Field Marshal, he holds that position for life. Therefore, in the summer of 1914, as war in Europe seemed inevitable, the government recalled French and he was appointed Commander in Chief of the British Expeditionary Force.

Sir John French's performance during his seventeen month tenure as Commander in Chief is generally acknowledged to have been a failure. Historians, such as Gary Sheffield, Robin Neillands and Richard Holmes all point to his unsuitability to hold this position in the first place. His personality as a man who held grudges; listened too much to the opinions of others; acted impetuously and yet suffered from severe guilt about the consequences of his decisions, meant that he lacked the detached, forceful and decisive nature required to see Britain and her allies through the war.

Sir Douglas Haig replaced French as Commander in Chief of the British Army in December 1915. French then returned to England. He never forgave Haig for his behind-the-scenes machinations and what had once been a close friendship deteriorated into mutual dislike. In January 1915, French was made Viscount French of Ypres and became Commander in Chief of Home Forces. This was a position he held until May 1918, when he was appointed Lord Lieutenant in the still greatly troubled Ireland. French had begun an affair with Mrs Winifred Bennett in 1916, following several other extra-marital relationships before the war and she frequently visited him in Ireland, as Eleanora had remained in England. French stayed in Ireland, through difficult and violent times, until May 1921, when he was replaced by Lord Edmund Talbot.

This was to be his last official position, although his retirement was by no means quiet and he retained a keen interest in military matters. His, by now strained, relationship with his family took the form of estrangement from all but his younger son, Gerald and, although French continued to live life to the full, his affair with Winifred Bennett also faded.

Sir John French died at Deal in Kent on 22nd May 1925, following a short battle with cancer. His funeral, a few days later, was held at Westminster Abbey and Haig was one of the pall-bearers. Thousands paid their respects as the gun carriage carrying his coffin processed through the streets. The war which French fought took everyone by surprise - the advances in weaponry alone meant that this was warfare on a scale never before experienced. French, a brilliant and daring cavalry officer, was, quite simply, unsuited to hold the position into which he was thrust in the summer of 1914.

CRITICAL ANALYSIS

PORTRAYAL OF CHARACTERS

By today's standards, all of the characters portrayed in *Oh What a Lovely War* are stereotypical: the arrogant Germans, the haughty French and the disdainful British generals and leaders are caricatures of their perceived national attributes. The generals are all seen to be bumbling, inept, buffoons, more concerned with their own careers and reputations than with the welfare of their men, or even the conduct of the war. The ordinary soldiers and nurses are portrayed sympathetically but civilians are treated more harshly: depicted as either profiteers or as women gleefully goading men into joining up. While such characterisations are representative of a proportion of those concerned, this is by no means a balanced view of the First World War.

Naturally, there were generals and politicians who did not care about anything except themselves, just as there were profiteers and women bearing white feathers, but there were just as many caring individuals of all ranks and stations in life. For example, some factory owners looked only at the money they could make, while others personally ensured that the families of their workers who had gone to fight, were well cared for in their absence.

In their initial conversation, Sir John French, Sir Henry Wilson and General Lanrezac try to put across each of their country's perspectives, despite the obvious language and cultural barriers. Each blames the other for any problems but all is 'solved' by Sir John French awarding Lanrezac with a medal on behalf of the King! This, and later, representations of Sir John French show him as incompetent and self-righteous.

At the dance, all of the officers are shown to be preoccupied with the advancement of their own careers to the point where the conduct of the war is not discussed at all. They are more interested in social climbing and appearances. The ladies who accompany them are seen to be shallow and narrow-minded - boasting about having joined the VAD, but only because the uniform is flattering!

The representation of Sir Douglas Haig is that of a bungling butcher, happily sending men to their deaths, whilst praying to at least be allowed victory before the Americans arrive to steal his thunder. This was a popularly held opinion at the time of the play's production and, in some quarters, remains so today. However, recent historians have posed a valid question: who else could have done the job, and would they have done it differently?

It must be remembered, when studying this play that it is a product of its time. The Second World War was over, but the 1960s saw a resurgence of interest in the earlier conflict previously known as the Great War. It is reputed that one of the reasons behind the retrospective criticism of the conduct of the First World War was the number of casualties caused during the war of 1939-1945. The figures for the numbers of victims of both conflicts vary from source to source, but it would certainly be fair to say that the First World War cost at least double the number of British lives to the Second World War. These figures refer only to military casualties, but even when civilians are included, the difference remains enormous. Many people began to question why the First World War had necessitated such wholesale slaughter. In addition, the use of conscription, particularly in the formation of the Pals Battalions of the First World War ensured that the huge loss of life continued to influence many families and society in general.

Historians and other interested parties began to write books which were very critical of the management of the First World War and the Generals in particular came in for vast amount of, frequently vitriolic, disapproval. Among these was *The Donkeys* by Alan Clark which was published in 1961 and formed a scathing attack on those who led the British Army in the First World War. Even at the time, other historians criticised the bias demonstrated in this book, but it was followed by many others along similar lines. In more recent years, the tide has turned and some historians are keen to defend the conduct of the First World War. These two uncompromising sides remain fixed in their viewpoint, although there are some writers who manage to present a more balanced viewpoint. This difference of opinion, almost a hundred years after the event, demonstrates the strength of feeling which this subject can provoke, even today.

In 1963, when *Oh What a Lovely War* was first performed, however, the vast majority were firmly on the side of the Donkeys - especially in light of the recent Cuban Missile Crisis. In brief, the Soviet Union, anxious that the USA had the greater nuclear firepower, colluded with the Cuban leader, Fidel Castro and arranged to place Soviet nuclear weapons on the island. Secret missile installations were hurriedly built in the summer of 1962, which came to the attention of the US government, when spotted in reconnaissance photographs. President Kennedy placed a naval blockade around Cuba to prevent the arrival of more Soviet weaponry, then on 22nd October 1962, he publicly announced the presence of these weapons and the blockade, as well as the positioning of 125,000 troops in Florida in anticipation of a possible invasion of Cuba. He declared that any strike by the Soviets would be deemed an act of war against the USA and demanded that all Soviet missiles must be removed from Cuban soil. Over the following days, tensions mounted across the world as, behind the scenes, the diplomats tried frantically to avert a major crisis. On 28th October, this was achieved when the Soviet leader Nikita

Khrushchev announced that he would sanction the removal of his country's weapons if the USA promised not to invade Cuba. This short crisis had revealed how easy it would be for the world to, once again, slide into war, but with the advent of nuclear weapons, such a war would have entirely different consequences.

Into this heightened tension, came the ground-breaking television satire, *That Was The Week That Was* which provided an irreverent look at political, domestic and foreign affairs. This programme, which first aired within a month of the Cuban Missile Crisis, attacked authority with the use of cutting satire, mixed with songs and sketches - a similar format to Joan Littlewood's production of *Oh What a Lovely War*. The whole point of programmes like TW3 (as it became known) was to question the 'establishment' perspective and, in this context, coupled with the perceived view of the First World War, which prevailed at the time, the representation of the characters in *Oh What a Lovely War* makes more sense. After all, to place too much emphasis on the reality of these characters and provide a completely balanced and unbiased viewpoint would, quite simply, not be very funny.

THE REPRESENTATION OF THE WAR

The subject of *Oh What a Lovely War* is the needless waste of life which typifies many peoples' perspectives of the Great War and its consequences. It is also a carefully worked piece of anti-establishment propaganda - in which the plight of those involved in the First World War happens to play a part. The entire first act depicts the causes and first few months of the conflict, showing the initial euphoria, the call-to-arms, lack of forward planning and the Christmas Truce. The second act then speeds through the remainder of the war, focusing mainly on the Somme, with barely a mention of Passchendaele, the American entry or the final few months of the war, leading to the Allied victory. So, it soon becomes clear that historical accuracy and impartiality is not the point of this play: rather it is to demonstrate the futility of it all; the incompetence of the 'lions' and nobility of the 'donkeys', or, put another way, the working class triumph over adversity and their upper-class masters.

Oh What a Lovely War uses biting satire to highlight the themes of the waste, the loss of life and the heartlessness of the First World War, exacerbated by callous and inept generals and leaders. By portraying these, usually serious and occasionally harrowing, themes in a satirical manner, the audience of the play is forced to question their own views and opinions. This is achieved by the use of irony - after all it feels quite insensitive to be laughing and singing, while continually reading in the background about millions of deaths, but this is exactly what the audience is forced to do.

Throughout the play the 'newspanel' highlights major events, paying particular attention to the number of casualties and how much, or little, ground has been gained for their sacrifice. This provides a continuous thread in the play, reminding the audience of the reality, as opposed to the parody which is being performed. The use of this device is essential to reinforce the serious element, giving a realistic air to the statistics which contrasts with the surreal aspects of the acting, singing and dancing.

The instances of futility in this play are too numerous to mention, but probably the most notable is the scene where the Irish soldiers are trapped in No Man's Land, unable to advance or retreat. The British guns start firing at them and every man who tries to get back and warn the artillery, is shot by a sniper. Although these men quickly come to understand their fate, they continue in a lighthearted manner to try and escape their predicament, despite the fact that this is a pointless exercise. The calibre and attitude of these men can be contrasted with the conversations between the senior officers. In particular, right at the beginning of the play, there is a meeting between Sir John French and Lanrezac, where neither of them understands the other and yet they carry on making war plans in a haphazard and disorganised fashion.

The action continually changes between the earnest and worthwhile, yet wasted soldiers, the heartless generals, the uncaring women and the profiteers. This technique is a not very subtle means of reminding the audience of the lack of organisation or forward planning which, the play purports, led to the high human cost of the First World War. In other words, by being chaotic and straying from the conventional ideas of theatre production, the play itself represents the futility of the war. The question is: does it also provide a fair representation of the First World War, or is its stance simply too biased to be taken seriously?

Very few would disagree that the level of casualties was unprecedented and many would argue that such a vast loss of life was also avoidable. Having taken the decision to become involved in the conflict, loss of life became inevitable, but a less predictable element was the number of casualties that would be involved. Most politicians and army leaders anticipated a short war and this was a feeling which filtered down to the general population, giving rise to the anticipation that it would 'all be over by Christmas'. This helped to fuel the initial euphoria and many young men joined up simply because they did not want to miss out on the fun! There was, however, a notable exception to this idea: Lord Kitchener expected a long drawn-out conflict and, right from the outset of the war, he began to make plans for a massive expansion to the army.

Despite all of his preparations, not even Kitchener anticipated the way in which this war would be fought. In 1914, the idea that both sides would effectively remain in the same place - a trench system stretching from the coast in Belgium to the Swiss border - seemed fanciful. The men who were now leading Britain's army had fought their wars very differently. Gone were the days of cavalry charges with lance and sword. These had been replaced by heavy artillery, machine guns, aircraft and, eventually tanks, and the leaders of Britain's new army had to learn how to do battle both with, and against these new technologies. In addition, the army itself had changed from a small, regular force of roughly 100,000 men, to a largely civilian body numbering in excess of 2,000,000 by the end of the war. Such were the elements with which the generals of the day had to contend.

Oh What a Lovely War shows the generals, without exception, as incompetent, uncaring and arrogant, enjoying life behind the lines, while their men fight and die in the trenches. While mistakes were certainly made - such as the prolonging of certain battles when it should have been clear that nothing was being achieved - not all of the generals can have been incompetent, or the Allies, quite simply, would not have won the war. In addition, while some might argue that the generals should have been closer to the front lines, this is clearly not practical. A general needs to be able to see the 'bigger picture' and this would not be possible from the close confines of the front line, from where he would only be able to see a minute part of the battlefield.

Another charge of the play is the futile nature of the conflict and the aspect which seems to most ably demonstrate this element of the war and which is continually repeated throughout, is the lack of ground gained for the losses incurred. On the face of it, this would seem to be a fair point. For example, during the four months of the Battle of the Somme, there were over one million casualties (on both sides), yet the advance was only approximately 12 kilometres. However, unlike the Second World War - which would have been a fairly recent memory in 1963, when this play was first produced - the Great War was not always about gaining ground. Like it or not, this became a war of attrition; wearing down the opposing side. Whether it was necessary for so many to die to prove that neither side really had the ability - at that time - to win, is still a matter of conjecture.

The conduct of the High Command and staff officers during the First World War remains a matter of high historical debate. Neither side finds it possible to agree with the other and broadly speaking they fit into two categories: the 'literary' historians and the 'military' historians. The former section cite the poetry and literature of the time (and indeed of subsequent decades) to demonstrate the futility and horror of the war and the contemporary nature of much of this writing lends it credence. One must, however, temper this argument by acknowledging that the number of men (and women) who wrote about their experiences is minuscule compared to the number of people who took part. It is not that this detail makes their opinion less valid, simply that it does not necessarily make it typical.

It is also interesting to note that many of the soldiers who wrote poetry, or went on to write novels and memoirs were mainly concerned with the quality of the men and the friendships which they formed during their service. The nature of the poetry written during the war changed as the war progressed. Brooke and Grenfell for example, wrote enthusiastically patriotic verse, but they died in 1915. The watershed came with the Battle of the Somme, after which the tone of poetry essentially changed: no longer did men write about glory, but about waste, death and futility. Generally speaking, it is this latter type of poetry which is used to demonstrate the horrors of war - many students first experience of anything connected to the First World War is frequently the poems of Wilfred Owen.

The military historians, many of whom have a background from within the services, dismiss most of the poetry and literature as not sufficiently representative of the real situation or conduct of the war. Here, they may have a point: much of the literature, for example, was written by and about officers, rather than the ranking soldiers. The soldier-poet's viewpoint is, therefore, regularly dismissed by the military historians as they seek instead to demonstrate the successes of the war (which was, as they readily point out, a victory), the changing military tactics and the difficulties of leadership at such a time.

Some of these historians, such as Brian Bond and Gary Sheffield argue that they are losing the battle of attempting to explain the war, drowning in a sea of emotive literature. Their arguments are interesting - enlightening even - especially as regards the general public's purported inability to see beyond the popular culture of *Oh What a Lovely War* and *Blackadder Goes Forth*. These valid explanations, however, are done a great disservice by other historians who, in their efforts to prove their point, misrepresent the literary elements of the war. In the introduction to his *Mud, Blood and Poppycock*, for example, Gordon Corrigan implies that Siegfried Sassoon was mentally ill at the time that his Declaration was published, and that its contents offended the men of his regiment. In the first instance, while Sassoon may have been at Craiglockhart when his Declaration appeared in *The Times*, his sanity was never in question and he was certainly not a resident there when he *wrote* the statement. Secondly, there is no record of any offense being felt by those in his regiment. In fact, Joe Cottrell, the quarter-master of the First Battalion - with whom Sassoon had served - is reputed to have shown the statement to several officers who agreed that its author was imprudent, but courageous, which hardly sounds like their were grossly offended by his actions. Such inaccuracies and implications, of which these are just two, coming in an otherwise well-written and interesting book demonstrate the military historian's desire to simply disregard or blatantly misrepresent the literary element.

While neither side can - or should - entirely dismiss the other's viewpoint, there is another type of book which gives a third perspective. This is the sector which recounts the experiences of the soldiers, nurses and civilians who lived through that time. In recent years, there have been an increasing number of these books, being produced now, before there are none of these individuals left to tell their story. When one reads their descriptions of events, even allowing that their outlook is limited by their experience, one comes to realise that both the military and literary historians have valid positions. The literature of the time is vital in shaping ones understanding of the culture of that time; the feelings of society and the participants in the conflict. The military standpoint gives a more matter-of-fact, but no less important perspective to the war, without which none of the rest can really be given a true context. These books also make one grasp the notion that regardless of what the military historians aver, most of us cannot entirely remove emotion from the argument.

COMPARISON

THE USE OF SATIRE IN FIRST WORLD WAR LITERATURE

It has been argued that Joan Littlewood's satire *Oh What a Lovely War* is in poor taste, and it is not a true reflection of the time which it depicts. However, it is in fact, replicating a type of humour which was popular, not just when the play was first produced, but also during the war itself. Among students of First World War poetry, the work of Siegfried Sassoon stands out for its ironic mocking of authority, the establishment - especially the church - and the war in general. This style, which he first began to use, although not exclusively, in 1916, generally lulls the reader into a false sense of security, before delivering a hammer-blow in the final one or two lines. Examples of this technique can be seen in *The One-Legged Man, Glory of Women, Lamentations* and *To Any Dead Officer* to name but a few. Sassoon still continued to write lyrical verse, such as *Banishment* and *The Death Bed*, but even here, having described a soldier's death in dreamlike terms, he reminds the reader that the war goes on regardless, as in the distance, he can still hear the guns.

Sassoon was not alone in using this method of bringing his experiences of the war to a wider audience. Another such was Alan P. Herbert who served with the Royal Naval Division until invalided out in 1917. After the war, he went on to write for *Punch* magazine as well as producing novels in his own right. Between 1935 and 1950 he was a Member of Parliament and was knighted in 1945. His First World War poetry demonstrates his pride in his men and his country, as in *The German Graves*, which speaks of English soldiers tending enemy graves, in the hope that their German counterparts will do the same for the English dead. His sense of honour is clear in this poem, but in others, such as *After*

the Battle, while still honouring the men, he shows his distaste for
the senior commanders in the army in a more ironic verse. Here,
he displays a sense of anger at the attitude of Generals who send
men to their deaths from comfortable chateaux and then, when the
men return, wounded, tired and missing their lost comrades,
congratulate them on a job well done.

Looking just at these few examples, one can easily begin to see that
the main target for the poets' displeasure is the senior officers. It is,
therefore, hardly surprising that this feeling was not unique to the
poets and filtered into other contemporary 'literature'. This includes
the trench magazines, especially and most famously, the *Wipers
Times*. This magazine was first printed in February 1916 by men of
the 12th Battalion Sherwood Foresters. They had discovered a
printing press in an abandoned building near Ypres in Belgium and
decided to produce a journal. Captain F J Roberts served as the
magazine's editor and it was produced as often as the war and
paper supplies allowed. The name of the magazine changed from
time to time, depending upon where the men were stationed,
although eventually it became known as the *B.E.F. Times*, when the
censor decided that the title might give unnecessary information to
the enemy. Many of the contributors remained anonymous, but one
of the 'regulars' was the poet and author Gilbert Frankau.

The magazines consisted of articles, poems, advertisements, stories
and regular features. Almost all of these were treated with the same
irreverence, making use of in-jokes and puns. Reading these
magazines today, one realises how important it was for the men to
maintain a sense of humour, as almost every aspect of a soldier's life
comes under the scrutiny of the various contributors. The main
targets are the army rules and regulations, senior officers and those
on the home front - who are humorously dealt with by the use of
supposed 'letters to the editor' in which civilians are seen to be
making ridiculous suggestions as to the conduct of the war.

One common thread in both the *Wipers Times* and much of the poetry is that it was written for and about officers, rather than the ranks. These officers were quite often middle or upper class and wrote about army life in terms which only other soldiers could fully understand. Some of the funniest contributions are the 'advertisements' which vary from notices for 'bright, breezy and invigorating' land for sale at Hill 60, perfect for housebuilding and with excellent views of Ypres, to a regular advert which appeared in most issues, telling readers of the latest 'production' at Cloth Hall, which had by this time been virtually destroyed by shell-fire, and which is described as the 'best ventilated Hall in the town'. Such jokes must have made more sense to those who really understood the true nature of the places mentioned, but even today, one can appreciate this dark humour.

Looking through copies of the *Wipers Times*, it is not too hard to trace the direction which followed in the production of *Oh What a Lovely War*. The use of humour is of a similar type and is directed at similar targets: profiteers, senior army officers, the home front etc., although, it must be said that, the circumstances of the production of the *Wipers Times* give it greater authenticity and, therefore, make it even more humorous. After all, it is one thing to produce a satire on the conduct of the First World War from the relative safety of the 1960s, but quite another to write humorous articles while only 700 yards behind the front line.

In the late 1980's the writers of the *Blackadder* series took the First World War satire to the next level: television. Here we see Captain Edmund Blackadder's continuous attempts, throughout the six part series, to escape the trenches, aided and abetted by his companions Private S Baldrick, and Lieutenant The Honourable George Colthurst St. Barleigh. Meanwhile their future is dictated by General Sir Anthony Cecil Hogmanay Melchett and his adjutant Captain Kevin Darling from the safety of their chateau many miles behind the front line. The humorous escapades of Blackadder and his comrades brought the First World War to a new generation of television viewers, demonstrating the horror and stupidity of the conflict. As with all the other satires, the target of the humour is the senior officers: Melchett is, to put it mildly, psychotic and his staff officer, Darling, enjoys his safe desk-job until the final episode when he is reluctantly sent to the trenches so as not to 'miss out' on taking part in the final big push. In addition both *Blackadder Goes Forth* and *Oh What a Lovely War* have politically motivated anti-establishment messages. They both portray the ordinary soldier - who represents the people - being betrayed by the authorities, although in both cases the blame is firmly placed on the army leaders, rather than the government.

Both productions also share the theme of the futility of the war. *Oh What a Lovely War* uses the newspanel to demonstrate the lack of ground gained and the number of lives lost, while in one episode of *Blackadder Goes Forth*, General Melchett shows George the exact amount of land captured by the British - it measures seventeen square feet.

This series has been criticised for its biased misrepresentation of the senior officers and their conduct in the First World War. As the 'military' and 'revisionist' historians are at pains to point out: to show, for example, Sir Douglas Haig sweeping toy soldiers into a dustpan is simply not representative of his role. One could counter this argument by pointing out that *Blackadder Goes Forth* is a situation *comedy*, not a documentary and should be treated as such. When one looks back at the earlier *Blackadder* series, they all prove to be parodies of a period in time and the fourth series is no different. Except for one detail: the subject matter arouses a greater diversity of intense opinion than any of the others. For example, the first series, entitled *The Black Adder*, which was first shown in 1983, recounts an alternative version of the Wars of the Roses, changing the outcome and re-writing history and yet this series has not been afforded the same level of popular and critical attention as *Blackadder Goes Forth*. Instead it is treated as an anarchic historical comedy - which is what it is.

The problem really arises when historians, journalists and critics - not to mention the general public - take these satires out of context, and this has undoubtedly been done in the case of *Blackadder Goes Forth*. The television programme reaches a far wider audience than any of the literature or history books on this subject and, for some, this may be their only exposure to the First World War. The programme's influence has been widespread - it is now studied in schools; it is mentioned in many history books; excerpts are shown within other documentary television programmes. All of which goes to demonstrate that once something enters popular culture and receives sufficient attention, if it is discussed often enough in various places, it can take on a degree of alleged accuracy. In other words, the mere fact that the 'military' historians find it necessary to censure *Blackadder* for its misrepresentation of the war, might even be giving it more credibility.

APPENDIX

Ranks in the British Army during the First World War

This study guide and the plays discussed herein contain numerous references to the ranks of the British Army. We have provided here an outline of these ranks, with a brief explanation of their role.

OFFICERS

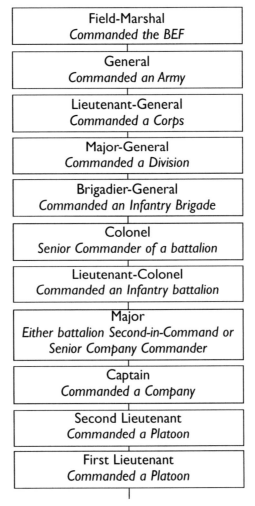

Field-Marshal
Commanded the BEF

General
Commanded an Army

Lieutenant-General
Commanded a Corps

Major-General
Commanded a Division

Brigadier-General
Commanded an Infantry Brigade

Colonel
Senior Commander of a battalion

Lieutenant-Colonel
Commanded an Infantry battalion

Major
Either battalion Second-in-Command or Senior Company Commander

Captain
Commanded a Company

Second Lieutenant
Commanded a Platoon

First Lieutenant
Commanded a Platoon

OTHER RANKS

**Regimental Sergeant-Major
or Warrant Officer Class I**
*Most senior non-commissioned officer
at battalion level.*

**Regimental Quartermaster-Sergeant
or Warrant Officer Class II**
*Senior Assistant to the Quartermaster
(who held the rank of Captain or Major).
Also acted as deputy to the RSM.*

Company Sergeant-Major
*Senior non-commissioned officer
at Company level.*

Sergeant
*This term usually applied to the
lowest rank of sergeant, with
additional words being used, such as
'Gunnery Sergeant' to denote higher
ranks and responsibilities.*

Corporal
Commanded a Section

Lance-Corporal
Second in Command of a Section

Private
Lowest ranking soldier

This table represents a guide as to the main ranks and roles in the British Army, as they stood during the First World War. Many other ranks existed, or came into being and the roles of some ranks changed or expanded as the war progressed.

FURTHER READING RECOMMENDATIONS FOR STUDENTS

Students are often expected to demonstrate a sound knowledge of the texts they are studying and also to enhance this knowledge with extensive reading of other texts within the subject. We have provided on the following pages a list of books, poetry, plays and non-fiction which, in our opinion, provide a good basic understanding of this topic. Those marked with an 'A' are suitable only for students of A-Level and above.

Novels

Strange Meeting by Susan Hill
Strange Meeting is a beautiful and moving book. It is the story of two young men, who meet in the worst circumstances, yet manage to overcome their surroundings and form a deep and lasting friendship. Susan Hill writes so evocatively that the reader is automatically drawn into the lives of these men: the sights, sounds and even smells which they witness are brought to life. It is a book about war and its effects; it is also a story of love, both conventional and 'forbidden'; of human relationships of every variety. This is a tale told during the worst of times, about the best of men.

Birdsong by Sebastian Faulks - A
This novel tells the story of Stephen Wraysford, his destructive pre-war love-affair, his war experiences and, through the eyes of his grand-daughter, the effects of the war on his personality and his generation. A central theme to this story is man's ability to overcome adversity: to rise above his circumstances and survive - no matter what is thrown in his path.

A Long Long Way by Sebastian Barry - **A**
This is a story about Willie Dunne, a young Irish volunteer serving
in the trenches of the Western Front. Willie must not only contend
with the horrors of the war, but also his own confused feelings
regarding the Easter uprising of 1916, and his father's disapproval.
This novel is about loyalty, betrayal, fear, wisdom and discovery.

A Very Long Engagement by Sebastien Japrisot
A story of enduring love and determination. Refusing to believe that
her lover can possibly have left her forever, Mathilde decides to
search for Manech whom she has been told is missing, presumed
dead. She learns from a first-hand witness, that he may not have
died, so she sets out on a voyage of discovery - learning not just
about his fate, but also a great deal about herself and human nature.

Regeneration by Pat Barker - **A**
This book is, as its title implies, a novel about the rebuilding of men
following extreme trauma. *Regeneration* is a story of man's
exploration of his inner being - his mind, feelings and reactions. It
details the effects of war on a generation of young men who,
because of their experiences, would no longer be able to live
ordinary lives.

The Return of the Soldier by Rebecca West
Written in 1918, this home-front novel gives a useful insight into
the trauma of war and societies reactions, as seen through the eyes
of three women. Chris Baldry, an officer and husband of Kitty,
returns home suffering from shell-shock and amnesia, believing that
he is still in a relationship with Margaret Allington - his first love.
Kitty, Margaret and Chris's cousin, Jenny, must decide whether to
leave Chris in his make-believe world, safe from the war; or
whether to 'cure' him and risk his future welfare once he returns to
being a soldier.

All Quiet on the Western Front by Erich Maria Remarque
Written from first-hand experience of life in the trenches, this novel
is the moving account of the lives of a group of young German
soldiers during the First World War. The fact that this, often
shocking, story is told from a German perspective demonstrates
the universal horrors of the war and the sympathy between men of
both sides for others enduring the same hardships as themselves.

Poetry

It is recommended that students read from a wide variety of poets,
including female writers. The following anthologies provide good
resources for students.

Poems of the First World War - Never such Innocence
Edited by Martin Stephen
Probably one of the most comprehensive and accessible anthologies
of First World War poetry. The notes which accompany each
chapter are not over-long or too complicated and leave the poetry
to speak for itself.

Lads: Love Poetry of the Trenches by Martin Taylor
Featuring many lesser-known poets and poems, this anthology
approaches the First World War from a different perspective: love. A
valuable introduction discusses the emotions of men who, perhaps
for the first time, were discovering their own capacity to love their
fellow man. This is not an anthology of purely homo-erotic poems,
but also features verses by those who had found affection and deep,
lasting friendship in the trenches of the First World War.

Scars Upon My Heart, Selected by Catherine Reilly
A collection of poems written exclusively by women on the subject
of the First World War. Some of the better known female poets are
featured here, together with the more obscure, and authors who

are not now renowned for their poetry, but for their works in other areas of literature.

Non-Fiction

Undertones of War by Edmund Blunden
Edmund Blunden's memoir of his experiences in the First World War is a moving, enlightening and occasionally humorous book, demonstrating above all the intense feelings of respect and comradeship which Blunden found in the trenches.

Memoirs of an Infantry Officer by Siegfried Sassoon
Following on from *Memoirs of a Fox-hunting Man*, this book is an autobiographical account of Sassoon's life during the First World War. Sassoon has changed the names of the characters and George Sherston (Sassoon) is not a poet. Sassoon became one of the war's most famous poets and this prose account of his war provides useful background information.
(For a list of the fictional characters and their factual counterparts, see Appendix II of *Siegfried Sassoon* by John Stuart Roberts.)

The Great War Generals on the Western Front 1914-1918 by Robin Neillands
Like many others before and since, the cover of this book claims that it will dismiss the old myth that the troops who served in the First World War were badly served by their senior officers. Unlike most of the other books, however, this one is balanced and thought-provoking. Of particular interest within this book is the final chapter which provides an assessment of the main protagonists and their role in the conflict.

The Western Front by Richard Holmes
This is one of many history books about the First World War. Dealing specifically with the Western Front, Richard Holmes looks

at the creation of the trench warfare system, supplying men and munitions, major battles and living on the front line.

Letters from a Lost Generation (First World War Letters of Vera Brittain and Four Friends)
Edited by Alan Bishop and Mark Bostridge
A remarkable insight into the changes which the First World War caused to a particular set of individuals. In this instance, Vera Brittain lost four important people in her life (two close friends, her fiancé and her brother). The agony this evoked is demonstrated through letters sent between these five characters, which went on to form the basis of Vera Brittain's autobiography *Testament of Youth.*

1914-1918:Voices and Images of the Great War by Lyn MacDonald
One of the most useful 'unofficial' history books available to those studying the First World War. This book tells the story of the soldiers who fought the war through their letters, diary extracts, newspaper reports, poetry and eye-witness accounts.

To the Last Man: Spring 1918 by Lyn MacDonald
This is an invaluable book for anyone studying *Journey's End* in particular, as it helps in the understanding of the personalities involved and the time through which they were living. As with all of Lyn MacDonald's excellent books, *To the Last Man* tells its story through the words of the people who were there. It is not restricted to a British perspective, but tells of the first few months of 1918 and their momentous consequences from every angle. The author gives just the right amount of background information of a political and historical nature to keep the reader interested and informed, while leaving the centre-stage to those who really matter... the men themselves.

GENERAL ADVICE TO STUDENTS

Although examinations can seem daunting, especially when the topic is as wide as First World War Literature, it is worth remembering the following simple tips:

• Be prepared. Read as much as possible beforehand; make sure you have revised well enough.

• Read the question. In other words, read it carefully, several times if necessary to be sure that you have a full understanding of what is expected. It is a very simple mistake to think you have understood the requirements only to find that you have completely misinterpreted them.

• Answer the question. Another common error is to get stuck in a train of thought and forget that what you are writing might not actually be answering the question in hand. You should stick to the topic required, even though you might have thought of a brilliant piece of analysis - if it doesn't relate to the question, it doesn't belong in your essay.

• Allow enough time. The examination paper will give you a guide as to how long to allow for each question. Think about the fact that you must plan your essay, deciding in advance how you want to approach the topic in hand. Don't forget to allow a few minutes at the end, just to check over what you have written.

Good luck!

BIBLIOGRAPHY

The First World War
by John Keegan

Chronology of the Great War, 1914-1918
Edited by Lord Edward Gleichen

To the Last Man: Spring 1918
by Lyn MacDonald

Rosebriars Trust
rosebriars.org.uk

Journey's End
by R C Sherriff

Strange Meeting
by Susan Hill

The Return of the Soldier
by Rebecca West

All Quiet on the Western Front
by Erich Maria Remarque

Birdsong
by Sebastian Faulks

Regeneration
by Pat Barker

A Long Long Way
by Sebastian Barry

Scars Upon My Heart
Edited by Catherine Reilly

Never Such Innocence
Edited by Martin Stephen

The British Expeditionary Force 1914-15
Bruce Gudmundsson

The Accrington Pals
by Peter Whelan

Pals on the Somme 1916
by Roni Wilkinson

The Somme
by Peter Hart

British Culture and the First World War
by George Robb

Not About Heroes
by Stephen MacDonald

**Siegfried Sassoon: The Making of a War Poet
A Biography 1886-1918**
by Jean Moorcroft Wilson

Siegfried Sassoon
by John Stuart Roberts

Siegfried Sassoon: A Biography
Max Egremont

Siegfried Sassoon: The War Poems
Arranged and Introduced by Rupert Hart-Davis

Siegfried's Journey
by Siegfried Sassoon

The Complete Memoirs of George Sherston
by Siegfried Sassoon

Wilfred Owen - War Poems and Others
Edited by Dominic Hibberd

The Poems of Wilfred Owen
Edited and with a memoir by Edmund Blunden

The War the Infantry Knew 1914-1919
by Captain J C Dunn

Goodbye to all That
by Robert Graves

Robert Graves - The Assault Heroic 1895-1926
by Richard Perceval Graves

Robert Graves - The Years with Laura 1926-1940
by Richard Perceval Graves

Robert Graves and the White Goddess 1940-1985
by Richard Perceval Graves

The Secret Life of Oscar Wilde
by Neil McKenna

Oscar Wilde
by Richard Ellman

Oh What a Lovely War
by Joan Littlewood's Theatre Workshop

The Little Field Marshal - a Life of Sir John French
by Richard Holmes

Haig's Command: A Reassessment
by Denis Winter

The War Generals on the Western Front 1914-1918
by Robin Neillands

The Pity of War
by Niall Ferguson

Forgotten Victory
by Gary Sheffield

The Unquiet Western Front: Britain's Role in Literature and History
by Brian Bond

Mud, Blood and Poppycock
by Gordon Corrigan

The Donkeys
by Alan Clark

The Wipers Times
A Facsimile Reprint of the Trench Magazines

OTHER GREAT WAR LITERATURE STUDY GUIDE TITLES

Great War Literature Study Guide Paperbacks:

Title	ISBN
All Quiet on the Western Front	978-1905378302
Birdsong	978-1905378234
Journey's End - GCSE	978-1905378371
Journey's End - A-Level	978-1905378401
Regeneration A-Level Study Guide	978-1905378395
Strange Meeting	978-1905378210
The Return of the Soldier	978-1905378357
Female Poets of the First World War - Vol. I	978-1905378258
War Poets of the First World War - Vol. I	978-1905378241

Great War Literature Study Guide E-Books:

Novels & Plays
All Quiet on the Western Front
Birdsong
Journey's End
Regeneration
Strange Meeting
The Return of the Soldier

Poets
Harold Begbie
Rupert Brooke
Female War Poets 1: WM Letts; M Postgate Cole; E Nesbit
Female War Poets 2: MW Cannan; K Tynan; C Mew
Female War Poets 3: N Cunard; I Tree; E Farjeon
Wilfrid Wilson Gibson

Julian Grenfell
Ivor Gurney
E A Mackintosh
John McCrae
Robert Nichols
Wilfred Owen
Jessie Pope
Isaac Rosenberg
Siegfried Sassoon
Charles Hamilton Sorley
Edward Thomas
Robert Ernest Vernède
Arthur Graeme West

Please note that e-books are only available direct from our Web site at www.greatwarliterature.co.uk and cannot be purchased through bookshops.